WHAT YOU NEED TO KNOW ABOUT

BIBLE PROPHECY

IN 12 LESSONS

MAX ANDERS

Publishers Since 1798

THOMAS NELSON PUBLISHERS
Nashville

Published in Nashville, Tennessee, by Thomas Nelson, Inc.

Library of Congress Cataloging-in-Publication Data

Anders, Max E., 1947–
    Bible prophecy / Max Anders.
    Includes bibliographical references.
    ISBN 0–8407–1938–8 (pbk.)
    1. Eschatology—Biblical teaching.   2. Bible—Prophecies.
I. Title.   II. Series.
BS680.E8A53   1997
220.1'5—dc21   96–52882
                                                                    CIP

Printed in the United States of America

2 3 4 5 6 7 8—01 00

CONTENTS

Introduction to the *What You Need to Know Series*　　iv

　　How to Teach This Book　　vi

Chapter　1　Why Study Prophecy?　　1

Chapter　2　What Is the Big Picture of Prophecy?　　15

Chapter　3　How Do We Explain Differences of
　　　　　　　Understanding in Prophecy?　　33

Chapter　4　What Are Some Key Terms Regarding "Future
　　　　　　　Things"?　　47

Chapter　5　What Are the Major Views on the Rapture?　　60

Chapter　6　What Are the Three Major Views on the
　　　　　　　Millennium?　　74

Chapter　7　What Final Judgment Awaits Humanity?　　93

Chapter　8　What Is Death?　　109

Chapter　9　What Is Hell?　　121

Chapter 10　What Is Heaven?　　137

Chapter 11　Will All Prophecies Be Fulfilled?　　151

Chapter 12　What Are the Universals upon Which We All
　　　　　　　Agree?　　161

Bibliography　　175

Master Review　　176

About the Author　　182

Introduction to the
What You Need to Know Series

You hold in your hands a tool with enormous potential—
the ability to help ground you, and a whole new generation of
other Christians, in the basics of the Christian faith.

I believe the times call for just this tool. We face a serious
crisis in the church today . . . namely, a generation of Christians
who know the truth but who do not live it. An even greater
challenge is coming straight at us, however: a coming generation of Christians who may not even know the truth!

Many Christian leaders agree that today's evangelical
church urgently needs a tool flexible enough to be used by a
wide variety of churches to ground current and future generations of Christians in the basics of Scripture and historic Christianity.

This guide, and the whole series from which it comes—the
What You Need to Know series, can be used by individuals or
groups for just that reason.

Here are five other reasons why we believe you will enjoy
using this guide:

1. *It is easy to read.*

You don't want to wade through complicated technical jar-
gon to try to stumble on the important truths you are looking
for. This series puts biblical truth right out in the open. It is
written in a warm and friendly style, with even a smattering of

humor here and there. See if you don't think it is different from anything you have ever read before.

2. It is easy to teach.

You don't have time to spend ten hours preparing for Sunday school, small group, or discipleship lessons. On the other hand, you don't want watered down material that insults your group's intellect. There is real meat in these pages, but it is presented in a way that is easy to teach. It follows a question-and-answer format that can be used to cover the material, along with discussion questions at the end of each chapter that make it easy to get group interaction going.

3. It is thoroughly biblical.

You believe the Bible, and don't want to use anything that isn't thoroughly biblical. This series has been written and reviewed by a team of people who are well-educated, personally committed Christians who have a high view of Scripture, and great care has been taken to reflect what the Bible teaches. If the Bible is unambiguous on a subject, such as the resurrection of Christ, then that subject is presented unambiguously.

4. It respectfully presents differing evangelical positions.

You don't want anyone forcing conclusions on you that you don't agree with. There are many subjects in the Bible on which there is more than one responsible position. When that is the case, this series presents those positions with respect, accuracy and fairness. In fact, to make sure, a team of evaluators from various evangelical perspectives has reviewed each of the volumes in this series.

5. It lets you follow up with your own convictions and distinctives on a given issue.

You may have convictions on an issue that you want to communicate to the people to whom you are ministering. These books give you that flexibility. After presenting the various responsible positions that may be held on a given subject, you will find it easy then to identify and expand upon your view, or the view of your church.

We send this study guide to you with the prayer that God may use it to help strengthen His church for her work in these days.

How To Teach This Book

The books in this series are written so that they can be used as a thirteen-week curriculum, ideal for Sunday school classes or other small-group meetings. You will notice that there only twelve chapters—to allow for a session when you may want to do something else. Every quarter seems to call for at least one different type of session, because of holidays, summer vacation, or other special events. If you use all twelve chapters, and still have a session left in the quarter, have a fellowship meeting with refreshments, and use the time to get to know others better. Or use the session to invite newcomers in hopes they will continue with the course.

All ten books in the series together form a "Basic Knowledge Curriculum" for Christians. Certainly Christians would eventually want to know more than is in these books, but they should not know less. Therefore, the series is excellent for seekers, for new Christians, and for Christians who may not have a solid foundation of biblical education. It is also a good series for those whose biblical education has been spotty.

Of course, the books can also be used in small groups and discipleship groups. If you are studying the book by yourself, you can simply read the chapters and go through the material at the end. If you are using the books to teach others, you might find the following guidelines helpful:

Teaching Outline

1. Begin the session with prayer.

2. Consider having a quiz at the beginning of each meeting over the self-test from the chapter to be studied for that day. The quiz can be optional, or the group may want everyone to commit to it, depending on the setting in which the material is

taught. In a small discipleship group or one-on-one, it might be required. In a larger Sunday school class, it might need to be optional.

3. At the beginning of the session, summarize the material. You may want to have class members be prepared to summarize the material. You might want to bring in information that was not covered in the book. There might be some in the class who have not read the material, and this will help catch them up with those who did. Even for those who did read it, a summary will refresh their minds and get everyone into a common mind-set. It may also generate questions and discussion.

4. Discuss the material at the end of the chapters as time permits. Use whatever you think best fits the group.

5. Have a special time for questions and answers, or encourage questions during the course of discussion. If you are asked a question you can't answer (it happens to all of us), just say you don't know, but that you will find out. Then, the following week, you can open the question and answer time, or perhaps the discussion time, with the answer to the question from last week.

6. Close with prayer.

You may have other things you would like to incorporate, and flexibility is the key to success. These suggestions are given only to guide, not to dictate. Prayerfully, choose a plan suited to your circumstances.

We should all be concerned about the future because we will have to spend the rest of our lives there.
■ **C.F. Kettering**

1

Why Study Prophecy?

*J*ane Eyre, written by Charlotte Brontë in 1847, is one of the most popular and enduring novels of the English language. It is a moving story of character, faith, love and redemption. The heroine, Jane Eyre, overcomes nearly insurmountable odds as a destitute orphan to achieve love, happiness and fulfillment as an adult.

Many movies have been made of *Jane Eyre*. Nearly all books are better than movies that are based on them, and that is no exception with *Jane Eyre*. However, there is a 1987 BBC version starring Timothy Dalton and Zelah Clarke that is quite faithful to the book.

I will never forget the first time I saw that version, especially one spooky scene that takes place in the middle of the night in a castle. A demented lady enters Jane Eyre's bedroom, and as Jane wakes and sees the ghastly specter moving in the room, the tension builds almost to the screaming point. The hideous form stalks about the room menacingly, and then it goes over to Jane, who is lying motionless and silent but with eyes wide open. Suddenly, a patch of candlelight reveals the demented face to Jane. The camera zooms in close for effect, and then the hideous intruder screams and lashes out at Miss Eyre. Of course, the movie director saw fit to accompany that explosive moment with a great crash of dissonant music. I almost toppled senseless to the floor.

The scene passed with no harm coming to Jane Eyre, and the movie continued, but that scene left my nerves vibrating like electrical wires in a strong wind.

Years later, my wife and I were watching the same movie with my brother and sister-in-law, who were seeing it for the first time. I had seen the movie several times since then, so it held none of the original suspense for me. I now knew the end from the beginning, so I could sit and enjoy it for the quality of the acting, script, and cinematography.

In this chapter we learn that . . .

1. Prophecy is the proclamation of the will of God, both present and future.
2. We study prophecy not only to learn about the future, but also to have it influence our daily lives.
3. There is a strong impression both among Christians and non-Christians that we are approaching the end of history on earth.

But out of the corner of my eye I noticed that my sister-in-law was showing the same signs of emotional strain which I had felt the first time I had seen the above, nerve-wracking scene. Her face was charged with tension. Her jaw was set, her mouth pursed tight, and her eyes were open wide and fixed on the scene. *Oh, this is going to be good,* I thought. *She is going to go ballistic.* I sat there biding my time, anticipating with pleasure, at my sister-in-law's expense, when the movie's gruesome goblin would make her move. I was not disappointed. My sister-in-law was stretched like a rubber band to the breaking point, and when the Great Moment came she jumped as though she had been jolted by electricity, and then she screamed unself-consciously.

Those who know the future have an advantage over those who do not.

It is certainly a flaw in my character, but I could not keep from laughing. I sat there, shoulders shaking, laughing the voiceless, breathy laugh of someone who cannot help it but doesn't want to get caught.

Later, I thought about the difference between a movie that you have seen only once and one that you have seen many times. When you see it again, you know the details and the ending, and that knowledge takes away the dread, the suspense, the emotional tension. I knew the story. My sister-in-law did not. I knew everything was going to turn out okay, even though the present circumstances were frightening. My sister-in-law did not. I knew there was going to be a happy ending. My sister-in-law did not. Obviously, knowing the future makes all the difference as to how we react to the present.

So it is with real life. Those who know the future, as revealed in the Bible, have a definite advantage over those who do not. Biblical prophecy tells us the future, and gives us strength, steadiness, and confidence in the midst of troubling circumstances; and it allows us to rest in the certainty of a happy ending to life and history. As someone once quipped about the Bible, "I read the last chapter, and we win!"

What Is Prophecy?

Prophecy is the proclamation of the will of God, both present and future.

A prophet is someone who speaks for God. We see prophets both in the Old Testament and the New Testament. They spoke for God in two different ways: forthtelling and foretelling. Forthtelling involved proclaiming the known word and will of God to His people; it could be understood as a "near-term" prophecy. Forthtelling included Bible teaching, evangelizing, and revival preaching, urging people to turn from sin and to live in righteousness, and warning what would happen to them if they did not repent. This was by far the major part of their ministry.

A second dimension to the ministry of a prophet was fore-telling, or "predicting the future." This could be understood as "distant-term" prophecy. These predictions were not the prophets' own predictions, however. The Scripture makes clear in 2 Peter 1:20–21 that "no prophecy of Scripture is of any private interpretation, for prophecy never came by the will of man, but holy men of God spoke as they were moved by the Holy Spirit." In other words, when God wanted to give information about the future to His people, He revealed that information to one of His prophets who then spoke that message to its intended audience.

When we talk about the subject of prophecy, it is usually this latter feature that is of greatest interest to us. We have a natural desire to know about the future, and when we learn that the Bible speaks about the future, our interest is stirred.

Why Study Prophecy?

We study prophecy not only to learn about the future but also to have it influence our daily lives.

The Bible makes it abundantly clear that God gives us information about the future not merely to satisfy our curiosity. Rather there are at least four reasons why God has given us prophecy.

Prophecy Encourages Godly Living

Perhaps the clearest point the Bible makes about prophecy is that information about the future is designed to purify us in the present. The apostle John wrote in his first epistle, "Beloved, now we are children of God; and it has not yet been revealed what we shall be, but we know that when He is revealed, we shall be like Him, for we shall see Him as He is. And everyone who has this hope in him purifies himself, just as He is pure" (1 John 3:2–3). When we think about the time when we shall see God, it stimulates us to purify ourselves in preparation to meet the One who is pure.

Knowing the future stirs us to holy living in preparation of meeting the One who is pure.

I'm embarrassed to say this, but on the rare occasions when my wife, Margie, is away for a few days, I'm pretty casual about housekeeping. I let the dirty dishes pile up in the sink. I leave Rice Krispie® crumbs on the counter where I spilled them. Magazines and books remain all over the living room and my dirty socks lay where they fell on the middle of the bedroom floor. But as the day for Margie's return draws near, I begin looking at everything through her eyes. I know her well enough to realize that what appears to me to be a comfortable, casual bachelor's pad will look like a pigsty to her. And usually just in the nick of time, I fly through the house cleaning and straightening and putting everything in its proper place. When she returns, the house is spotless and I'm exhausted!

The same thing in principle often happens to us in our relationship with God. We lose sight that we are going to die or that Jesus could return at any moment. So we begin acting as though we will live forever or that Jesus will never return. Dirty dishes pile up in our hearts. Clutter and junk accumulates in our minds. Dirty socks are left on the floor. Needless to say, God doesn't want us to live this way. And when we read in the Scriptures about the Lord's return, we are reminded that we need to get our house in order and to live each day as though He could return that day. Yes, one of the key purposes of prophecy is to encourage us to godly living.

Bible prophecy is a complex subject, however, and not easily mastered. It is easy to overstep our actual understanding of prophecy without realizing it. For example, I came to Christ in college during a fever pitch of interest in Bible prophecy and the end times. It was in the mid-1960s, and it seemed as if we were just beginning to understand some of the hidden things in the Scripture about the final events of history. Shortly after my coming to Christ, a book written about the end of the world sold millions of copies. It was so clear. The end was at hand. Bible teachers were putting two and two together, and one thing seemed certain to me. I would never see my fortieth birthday on earth.

Why I need to know the importance of studying prophecy

If I don't understand the importance of studying prophecy, I may not understand that Jesus is coming again and that I need to be ready. I may not have the motivation to let others know this. I may get lazy in my spiritual life, and I may neglect a part of the Bible that God surely revealed to me for a purpose. I may also miss the assurance the Lord provides through prophecy—the assurance that He is in control, that He loves me, and that He will take care of His children, no matter what the future holds.

Thirty years have come and gone. My fortieth birthday has come and gone. I'm still here. And this has made me become very cautious about exceeding what I really know about biblical prophecy.

It reminds me of the time when, as a new Christian, I encountered two people at a large religious gathering who seemed ready to fight each other over whether the earth was going to be destroyed by fire in the future. They were nose to nose, like a seasoned drill sergeant and a clumsy new recruit, except that they were both acting like the drill sergeant. Brows were furrowed in anger, neck veins were bulging, eyes were popping, and ungracious words were pouring like water from a fire hydrant.

Such attitudes over possible prophetic meanings reveal that Christians are missing the whole point of biblical prophecy and missing an opportunity to influence the world. The point of prophecy is not merely to satisfy our curiosity. Nor has enough prophetic information been given to us to let us **It is okay for Christians to hold different convictions about prophecy.** say with absolute confidence that we know exactly what's going to happen in the future. Certainly it is valid to discuss possible meanings and to hold personal convictions about them. But it is a complete collapse of the true purpose of prophecy when Christians alienate each other over the meanings of prophetic passages.

There are enough spiritually mature, well-educated and in

telligent people on many different sides of the prophetic issues, and this helps us see that we ought to treat responsible positions on prophecy with respect. We should never allow ourselves to degenerate into an attitude that wants to win a biblical argument at the expense of Christian character.

A second problem resulting from Christians feuding over prophecy is that it compromises our witness. The world looks at us and wonders what significance prophecy has for them. People are smart enough to realize that if Christian truth results in Christians fighting among themselves, then what value is there in biblical prophecy? Prophetic truth can be a powerful tool to encourage people to accept the other truths of Scripture, but usually only if the message is combined with a compelling Christian character. Therefore, as we study and discuss prophetic truth, as we come to our own convictions about it, and as we proclaim it, we must do so with a spirit of peace, love, and respect for other responsible positions. We must proclaim our message with a backdrop of credible Christian character.

Prophecy Gives Us Hope and Comfort

I will never forget my reaction when I learned, in the first days of my Christian life, that Jesus could return at any moment and that many other people also believed this, because the signs of the times suggested that He would. I was excited and disappointed at the same time. I was excited that I would never have to die a natural death and that I would live to see the climactic events of life on earth. But I was disappointed because I would never get to realize some of my dreams. My whole life lay ahead of me. I wanted to get married, have children, and be a success in life. I wanted Jesus to return, but not until I had enjoyed some of the things this world had to offer. When I had had the best of this world, then it could end; and then I could enjoy the best of the next world. I wanted it all.

Since then, I have tasted many of the successes and enjoyments that this world has to offer, and none of them in my opinion offers enough reward compared to what heaven will be like. And I can tell you now that I am ready for Jesus to return. I long for history to end and for a righteous eternity to begin. It is not that I do not enjoy life. The good things that I have enjoyed in life have been, in large measure, better and greater than I ever imagined they would be when I was young. But at the same time, the pain and disappointment has also been greater. In addition, I have begun to empathize with the pain and suffering of the world around me in a way I never did as an idealistic young man, as someone living in the most privileged country at the most privileged time in history.

Now, to me, one of the most precious passages in Scripture is Revelation 21:4, "And God will wipe away every tear from their eyes; there shall be no more death, nor sorrow, nor crying; and there shall be no more pain, for the former things have passed away."

When I assess the personal pain, both physical and emotional, that has come to me since the early days of my Christian faith, when I see the pain of loved ones, when I see pain of others, when I see the ghastly examples of man's inhumanity to man worldwide, when I see the pressure rising on global problems like an overheated pressure cooker, it is then that I read God's promises of an ultimate end to the ravages of sin, and I greet them like a rescue ship to one who is adrift on a life raft at sea. *Saved*, I think. *We will be saved!*

Truths about the end times and the events that transition us out of time and into eternity are no longer abstract truths that I am ambivalent about. Like the person lost at sea, I cling to the hope these truths give, and prophecy becomes meaningful. I believe prophecy often becomes more important to us as we see the end of life drawing near. When we wrestle with poor health or life-shattering circumstances or bitter disappointments, God's prophetic words of promise for our future assure us and strengthen us for faithful, joyful endurance.

A piece of graffiti says it well: *Life is hard and then you die.* That is the perspective of those who are not able to look to a time when wrong will be righted, when pain will cease and all will be well. Prophecy gives us that comfort, that peace, that hope. It lets us look into the future and learn that in the end God will set everything right and all will be well.

Prophecy Warns Us to Flee from the Wrath to Come

For those who have not received Christ as their personal savior, there is nothing to look forward to in death; just the opposite, death is to be greatly feared. Those who die without Christ pay the full penalty for their sins. Those who die in Christ are forgiven of their sins and Jesus takes their penalty. For that reason, it is a fearful thing to fall into the hands of an angry God. The apostle Paul wrote in Romans 1:18, "For the wrath of God is revealed from heaven against all ungodliness and unrighteousness of men . . ." Knowing this, we are warned, and we can flee from the wrath to come.

Prophecy Gives Us Confidence in God's Character and Sovereignty

I have a friend who has produced and directed several movies. He once told me that no matter how chaotic the movie appears to be on the screen, whether it is a fighting scene, a riot, or people fleeing in danger, nothing happens by accident. Everything on the screen is calculated and planned down to the last person and smallest action. Though things seem to be utterly out of control, the director has them solidly in control. Life is not a movie, but it does at times appear to be out of control. There are wars and rumors of wars. There are men committing acts of inhumanity against other men. There is famine. There are earthquakes. There are revolutions and uprisings. And yet through all this, God is working a good and perfect will. It may make no sense to us, but some day it will. The screen of our lives sometimes reveals a great deal of chaos, and yet when we see behind the scenes, when we see how the Great Movie was made, we will see that God had everything under control.

Without knowing biblical prophecy, life seems chaotic and meaningless.

If it were not for Scripture, we wouldn't have the faintest reason to believe this. Without prophecy showing us how history is marching from the beginning through a middle and to a conclusion that is predetermined, we could easily come to the conclusion that this life is chaotic and meaningless.

Psalm 103:19 says, "The Lord has established His throne in heaven, and His kingdom rules over all."

In Revelation 21–22, we read of a new heaven and a new earth, which God is going to institute at a predetermined time that only He knows. In this new heaven and in this new earth only righteousness will reign, and God will dwell among us. He will be our God and we will be His people. These statements of biblical truth and pictures of reality give us hope and confidence in the character and sovereignty of God.

Why Is There a Strong Interest in Prophecy?

There is a strong impression both among Christians and non-Christians that we are approaching the end of history on earth.

When I was a child I saw television images of Russian tanks and United States tanks facing each other ominously across the border of the city of Berlin before the Berlin Wall was erected. I remember vividly the television picture cutting to a full close-up of Nikita Khrushchev, the premier of the Soviet Union at the time, as he thundered, "Unless the United States is willing to get out of Berlin, war is inevitable!" I was terrified. I didn't know what the word inevitable meant and so I looked it up in the dictionary immediately. It meant that something was certain, unavoidable. I went to bed wondering whether or not the United States and the Soviet Union were going to go to war. I wondered whether or not nervous fingers would finally push the buttons that would plunge the world into nuclear nightfall.

There were other nights when I wondered the same thing, such as during the tense moments over the Cuban Missile Crisis, the Soviet invasion of Afghanistan, and the periodic violence in the Middle East. There was a profound sense of relief when the Soviet Union collapsed and Communism was repudiated. It was the general consensus of world watchers that the probability of nuclear war between the United States and Russia was significantly reduced. The world heaved a great sigh of relief. Many of us were momentarily lulled into thinking that the world was now a safe place.

And while the world is certainly a safer place, it is by no means safe. Though the threat of nuclear holocaust may be radically diminished, other threats loom ominously on the horizon. Widespread pollution of the environment and destruction of the rain forests may upset the balance of life on earth; and terrorists now have much greater opportunities to stockpile nuclear arms or insidious biological weapons. In addition, viruses and bacteria resistant to known medical treatment are springing up all over the world.

The problems the world faces seem so enormous, so serious, so insurmountable that people have a growing sense of uneasiness as to whether the world will find a way through the problems. The dramatic rise in technological capability, along with a decline in the moral inclination to use that technology for the benefit of humanity, has left people worldwide with a sense of impending crisis.

Certainly Christians are well advised not to become too specific about when Jesus will return and when the end of life on earth as we know it ceases. The Bible says that no one knows the day or the hour when Jesus will return. But Christians have embarrassed themselves repeatedly by ignoring that clear biblical admonition.

I will never forget when the church I was pastoring in the summer of 1988 became abuzz over a booklet titled *Eighty-eight Reasons Why the Rapture Will Be in 1988*. The book seemed on the surface to be well reasoned and well documented by an intelligent Christian who had put what he thought was two and two together to equal what he thought was four. The book was so compelling that many Christians who should have known better jumped on the bandwagon and said that the Rapture was going to happen that year.

Biblical prophecy brings comfort amidst the world's increasing pressures and problems.

It is now many years later and the Rapture obviously did not happen. But that didn't disturb the author of the booklet, who immediately saw how he had miscalculated; he then recalculated and said that the Rapture was going to happen in 1989. However, it didn't happen then either. This ought to have been enough to convince Christians that setting a date for the Rapture is a precarious business. However, when enough time passes, people forget and someone comes up with another dating scheme, and again Christianity ends up with egg on its face. To say that we cannot know the day or hour of Jesus' return is as clear as any statement in the Bible. This is not to say that we are not given a general indication of circumstances that will exist during the time of Jesus' return. For example, Jesus Himself gave us several illustrations that, I believe, along with many other Bible teachers, instruct us to be on the lookout for signs that might indicate the coming of the end. For instance, Jesus and His disciples had just left the temple and they asked Jesus if He would tell them what would be a sign of His coming and the sign of the end of the age. And while Jesus warned them not to get duped by bad information, He did say that as the lightning comes from the east and flashes to the west so will the coming of the Son of Man be (Matthew 24:27). This may mean that it will be as quick as a flash of lightning.

However, He then adds that they should learn a parable from the fig tree. "When its branch has already become tender, and puts forth its leaves, you know that summer is near. So, also, when you see all these things, know that it is near, at the very doors. Assuredly, I say to you, this generation will not pass away until all these things are fulfilled" (24:32–34). "These things" refers to all of the events that He described to them in Matthew 24:4–26. He then says, "but of that day and hour no one knows, not even the angels of heaven, but my Father only. . . . Therefore, you also be ready, for the Son of Man is coming at an hour when you do not expect Him" (24:36, 44).

Although it is not possible for us to know the exact day or hour of Jesus' return, there are signs that it is approaching. Because of this, we **Biblical prophecy can turn pessimists into optimists.** can be alert, ready, and watching; and we are to be responsive, which will motivate us to to help as many people as possible to be ready.

Conclusion

We all long to know the future. For some of us, it may be something as simple as shaking the packages under the Christmas tree to guess their contents. For others it may be something as weighty as consulting a spirit medium to try to learn about life and death. Television is filled with commercials for psychics and mediums promising to tell the future of your relationships and finances. The horoscope is found in thousands of our nation's newspapers.

It is particularly intriguing to walk through the grocery checkout counters in December to see tabloid headlines screaming absurd predictions for the coming year. A parade of psychics marches out on a limb and promptly saws it off behind them, so absurd are their predictions, which virtually never come to pass. Nevertheless, Americans rush to buy them for what might be a glimpse of the unseen and the unknown.

Surreptitiously, I recently purchased one of these publications and read the predictions for next year. A baby would be

born in space; the South Pacific island nation of Tonga would
stun the world by launching a spacecraft to the moon; a massive
new radio telescope covering half the Nevada desert would discover intelligent life on a planet circling a small star only seven
light-years from earth. Five million senior citizens enraged over

**Jesus knows that
our curiosity about
the future is
important.**

cuts in their government subsidies would
march on Washington and occupy the House of
Representatives (how five million additional
people would fit into Washington, D.C. and the
House of Representatives was not explained).

A scientist would say he's lived in a Bigfoot village hidden in the
Canadian Rockies for more than two years. Astronomers using
special film and the Hubble Space Telescope would capture pho-
tos of angels a million miles tall playing catch among the stars!

I can't wait.

What fuels this intrigue? First, I think there is a natural curiosity to know the "rest of the story," as Paul Harvey tells us. If
you hear the setup for a joke, you want to hear the punch line. If
you hear the first half of a story, you want to know how it comes
out.

Beyond that, if something good is going to happen to us,
perhaps we want to know it so we can begin enjoying it as soon
as possible. And, if something bad is going to happen to us, perhaps we want to know it in case there is something we can do to
avoid it or prepare for it.

Much of the visible curiosity about the future is found in the
world of tabloid newspapers and television psychics. But curiosity about the future is by no means confined to those arenas. It is
universal among all people. Even Jesus' disciples were curious.
In Matthew 24, a passage we looked at earlier (see also Luke 21),
Jesus' disciples remarked about the beauty of the temple. Jesus
said, "Do you not see all these things? Assuredly, I say to you,
not one stone shall be left here upon another, that shall not be
thrown down" (verse 2). And as they arrived at the Mount of
Olives, the curiosity of His disciples got the better of them, and
they asked, "Tell us, when will these things be? And what will be
the sign of Your coming, and of the end of the age?" (verse 3).

Jesus did not think that their questions were inappropriate.
He even began telling them about some of the signs of His coming and of the end of the age. Since that day, all God's people
have been wondering the same thing: when will the end of the

age come, and what signs will precede it? Throughout church history, theories and interpretations have abounded and been revised; so, too, today. It is appropriate, then, that in a study of the basics of Christianity, we look closely at the subject of Bible prophecy.

Speed Bump!

Slow down to be sure you've gotten the main points of this chapter.

Question
Answer

Q1. What is prophecy?

A1. Prophecy is the proclamation of the will of God, both *present* and *future.*

Q2. Why study prophecy?

A2. We study prophecy not only to learn about the future, but also to have it influence our daily lives.

Q3. Why is there a strong interest in prophecy?

A3. There is a strong impression both among Christians and non-Christians that we are approaching the end of history on earth.

Fill in the Blank

Question
Answer

Q1. What is prophecy?

A1. Prophecy is the proclamation of the *will* of God, both _____ and _____ .

Q2. Why study prophecy?

A2. We study prophecy not only to learn about the future, but also to have it _____ our daily lives.

Q3. Why is there a strong interest in prophecy?

A3. There is a strong impression both among Christians and non-Christians that we are approaching the _____ of history on earth.

For Further Thought and Discussion

1. How much thought have you given to the end of the world? Have you ever thought that the world might come to an end?

2. Have you thought much about dying? Have you assumed that you would die, or did you think that the end of the world might come first?

3. When you think about the possibility of Christ's coming back to earth in your lifetime, does it cause you to want to live a better life? What areas of your life do you want to see improved before He returns? What keeps you from improving those areas?

What If I Don't Believe?

1. If I don't believe that Christ is coming again, I may be inclined to live as though He will never return. I probably think that I will never have to face Him and be held accountable for my life. It will be easier to go on living as though God doesn't really exist.

2. I give less weight to Scripture than God does, because He gave the prophetic passages of Scripture.

3. I become less able to understand the turbulence of modern times and take comfort that God is in control.

4. I am severely limited in my ability to help others make sense out of the world, and I cannot make a credible defense of the Christian faith.

For Further Study

1. Scripture
Several passages speak of the importance of prophecy in our lives. They include:

- 1 John 2:28–3:3

- 2 Peter 2:20–21

- Matthew 24:44

- Revelation 20–21

2. Books
Several other books are helpful in studying this subject further. They include:

Doomsday Delusions, C. Marvin Pate and Calvin B. Haines, Jr.
Contemporary Options in Eschatology, Millard Erikson
The Meaning of the Millennium: Four Views, Robert Clouse, ed.

No man ever sank under the burden of the day. It is
when tomorrow's burden is added to the burden of
today that the weight is more than a man can bear.
Never load yourself so. If you find yourself so loaded,
at least remember this: it is your own doing, not
God's. He begs you to leave the future to him, and
mind the present.
■ George MacDonald

What Is the Big Picture of Prophecy?

I'm not generally a big fan of the parades that are seen on television from Thanksgiving through New Year's Day each year. There is one exception, however: the Rose Bowl Parade in Pasadena, California. Each year I am amazed anew at the size, complexity, and intricacy of the floats. It taxes my imagination to think that everything on every single float is some kind of plant matter. One float might be a 100-foot-long replica of the space shuttle, revealing size, power, and technology, while the next might be a 30-foot-tall replica of a South American parrot, displaying brilliant colors and delicate feathers. The creativity, the skill, and the monumental amount of work necessary to create the floats in the short time they have to keep the plant matter from wilting or spoiling makes this a spectacular example of American culture and ingenuity.

Along the parade route is a large grandstand with judges, dignitaries, VIPs, and television cameras. From there, people watch the array of flowered jewels float past for several hours.

And yet, whether one is sitting in the grandstand or watching on television, he can only see a small part of the parade at any one time. He can only see the floats that have just passed, the float that's in front of him, and the floats that are about to pass by. If the parade is, for example, halfway through, there may be a mile or more of floats that he has seen and now only has a memory of. Another mile of floats is still to come, and he has no idea what these might be since he has not seen them. But the people in the Goodyear blimp high above

---

In this chapter we learn that . . .

1. Creation is the beginning of the universe and human life.
2. A covenant is a binding agreement between two individuals, and God has embarked on a series of agreements with humanity.
3. Christ is the fulfillment of God's Old Testament covenant promises for Messiah to come to redeem humanity.
4. The church is the totality of all believers in Jesus; they are to carry out His will on earth until He comes again.
5. Consummation is the completion of God's redemptive plan.

Pasadena can see the entire parade simultaneously. In a sense, there is no "part way through the parade" for those in the blimp. It sounds paradoxical, but they can "look ahead" to see what's coming up and they can "look back" at what's already been. And they can do this as easily as those stuck in the grandstand who see only "the present." Simply put, those in the blimp see past, present, and future.

This is very much the way God sees history. He can see the past, the present, and the future simultaneously. We are locked into seeing the small slice of history in which we live. The **God can see all history—past, present, future— simultaneously.** past is already gone; we cannot see it, though we may have a dim memory of it. The future has not yet happened so, therefore, we cannot see it either. All we can see is the present. Seen this way, history is that part of the parade which has already happened. The present is that part of the parade in front of the grandstand where we are sitting. The future is that part of the parade still to come.

Because God sees and knows all things, He sees the entire parade—past, present, future—simultaneously. The future, therefore, is no more of a mystery to Him than the past. This is a helpful image when thinking about biblical prophecy. And it is especially helpful to consider all the elements of the parade of time in which humanity finds itself. While watching the Rose Bowl Parade, you might see several floats followed by a marching band, followed by more floats, followed by a troop of Arabian horses. Just so, there is a sequence of events in the parade of time. It is by looking at this sequence that we can gain an overall picture of prophecy.

God's parade of history, as it were, includes five floats. The float of creation, the float of covenant, the float of Christ, the float of the church and the float of consummation. As each of these floats passes by the grandstand of the "present," we see the outworking of the will of God in relationship to humanity.

What Is Creation?

Creation is the beginning of the universe and human life.

The first float to pass the grandstand of human history is "creation." The Bible says that in the beginning God created the heavens and the earth. "The beginning" there refers to the beginning of time as we know it. Exactly what existed before the creation of the universe and the world as we know it today, we do not know for sure. We know that God is eternal, meaning that He has always existed and, therefore, existed before the point of creation; but what He did and what went on before that point of creation, we are not told. While the Bible does not give us a great deal of information about the creation of the universe and the world and time as we know it today, it does give us beginning points for understanding some of it. As we investigate those beginning points, it is helpful to ask several questions.

What Did God Create?

Since God is the only uncreated thing in the universe, we can look at whatever exists outside of God and know that it was created by Him. For example, we see that angels were created before the creation of the world (Psalm 148:2, 5; Job 38:4–7). Then God created the universe and the world as we know it today, as we read in Genesis 1. In addition to having created the universe and the world, God also created everything that inhabits the world including all of the plants and all of the animals.

Finally, God created humanity to exist on a level above anything else. Humans were created not only in the image of God (Genesis 1:26) but also to have dominion over the rest of creation on earth (Genesis 1:28). Theologians endlessly debate exactly what it means to have been created in the image of God, but it

---

Why I need to know this

I need to know the big picture of prophecy, or else I will fail to understand God's plan, and very possibly lose hope and confidence in it.

does not seem to mean a physical image or likeness because God
is spirit (John 4:24). The Bible also makes it clear that humans
have a spirit (James 2:26). It is this spiritual makeup of humanity
that appears to have been created in the image of God (Genesis
2:7).

How Did God Create?

Theologians say that God created *ex nihilo*, which is Latin,
meaning "out of nothing." It means that God created that which
now exists, out of that which did not exist. He created something
out of nothing. We see this clear concept from the creation narra-
tive in the Book of Genesis. Beginning with the first verse in
Genesis, we read, "In the beginning God created the heavens
and the earth." Then beginning in verse three, the writer of Genesis goes on to explain how God created the heavens and the
earth. Verse three reads, "Then God said, 'Let there be light.' And
there was light." The simple deduction is that the light that existed came about as a result of God's speaking. Nothing else.
God spoke creation into existence out of nothing that existed before.

This is, of course, unlike anything that humans have ever
seen or can even conceive. And because this creation, *ex nihilo*,
was done by a good God, it comes as no surprise to learn
throughout the first chapter of Genesis that God pronounced
everything He created as "good."

Why Did God Create?

One of the great questions theologians love to debate is,
"*Why* did God create?" There are many speculations and partial
answers as to why He created, but the Bible nowhere gives us a
complete and clear answer to that question. If God is perfect
within Himself, which implies that He has no need of anything
outside Himself, then the question is, "Why then did God create
anything at all?"

People have erroneously said that God was lonely and He
needed other companions to keep Him company. Others have
suggested that He was bored; perhaps He did not have enough
to do, so creating the universe and humanity gave Him some
toys to play with. Others have cynically suggested that God is a
cosmic egomaniac, that He wanted to create a race of beings who
would grovel at His feet for eternity. However, if the Bible is

true—if God is in fact a perfect Being, complete within Himself—then none of these speculations are valid.

The Bible gives evidence of more than one reason why God created. The first is that God created for His glory. In Isaiah 43:6–7 God speaks of His sons and daughters whom He had created "for My glory." And, not only humanity, but also the entire physical universe exists to show God's glory. The psalmist wrote, "The heavens declare the glory of God; and the firmament shows His handiwork" (Psalm 19:1). The song of worship in Revelation 4 speaks of the relationship between God's creation of the universe and the fact that He is worthy to receive glory from His creation:

> You are worthy, O Lord,
> To receive glory and honor and power;
> For You created all things,
> And by Your will they exist and were created.

But while God created the universe for His glory, it is also clear that He takes delight in it just as we take delight in things we create. Since humanity is created in God's image, and since it is clear that humanity delights in creating, then it also seems clear that the human desire to create might be part of the very nature and character of God. People with artistic skill, whether it is in music or painting or writing or speaking or singing, or decorating or cooking, or inventing, or making things—they all seem incapable of *not* creating. As such, they may be reflecting the nature and character of God.

To gain additional insight as to why God created, we can look at the theme of love that runs throughout the Bible. The Bible says that God is love (1 John 4:8) and that when humanity was separated from God by sin, it was His love that motivated Him to send Jesus to die for our sins (John 3:16). The Bible also says that of the great virtues of faith, hope, and love, the greatest is love (1 Corinthians 13:13).

It is not difficult to imagine that God's love is so overflowing and so abundant that He wanted to create people—a unique class of creation—whom He could love and who would choose to love Him in return. James Packer, in his book, *God Has Spoken*, has written that

> the truly staggering answer which the Bible gives to this question is that God's purpose in revelation is to make friends with us. It

was to this end that He created us rational beings, bearing His image, able to think and hear and speak and love; He wanted there to be genuine personal affection and friendship, two-sided, between Himself and us—a relationship, not like that between a man and his dog, but like that of a father to his son, or husband to his wife. Loving friendship between two persons has no ulterior motive; it is an end in itself. And that is God's end in revelation. He speaks to us simply to fulfill the purpose for which we were made; that is, to bring into being a relationship in which He is a friend to us, and we to Him, He finding His joy in giving us gifts and we finding ours in giving Him thanks (50).

The *Westminster Shorter Catechism* states that the "chief end of man is to glorify God and enjoy Him forever." This reiterates the reciprocal relationship which God appears to have intended in creating humanity. It is a relationship of love and of glory: God's loving us and our giving Him glory.

God's love remains unchanged after the fall and so redeems us.

When God created Adam and Eve, they were without sin. But as we see in Genesis 3, Adam and Eve sinned against God. This sin brought into the world all the pain, all the evil, and all the suffering that has ever been experienced, that is now being experienced, and that will ever be experienced. The calamitous results of Adam's and Eve's decision to sin is often called "the Fall" of humanity. However, God's love for humanity remained unchanged even after the Fall, and He instituted a way to be redeemed: to have our sins forgiven, to be made new, to be recreated in the righteousness of Jesus and restored to a life of unending fellowship with God.

The acts leading to redemption and following it are the additional floats which now must pass the grandstand of time. And we now turn our attention to the second float, which is "covenant."

What Is Covenant?

A covenant is a binding agreement between two individuals, and God has embarked on a series of agreements which He makes with humanity.

As a result of the Fall, humanity now finds itself in a precarious position. We were created by God for righteous fellowship and harmony with Him. Yet because of our sin, we have been separated and cut off from God and we have no capacity within ourselves to correct the situation. But the same love that motivated God to create in the first place now motivates God to redeem us. A covenant is a binding promise, a legal agreement, a formal contract. After the fall, God offered us a covenant that would bring about a partial restoration of His intention for us here on earth *and* a complete and full restoration of His intention for us in eternity. God promises to forgive and to redeem us if we will simply turn to Him in faith and ask Him to.

In both the Old and the New Testaments people are saved by faith in God. We read in Romans 4:2–3:

> For if Abraham was justified by works, he has something to boast about, but not before God. For what does the Scripture say? "Abraham believed God and it was accounted to him for righteousness."

Again, we read in 4:13:

> For the promise that he would be the heir of the world was not to Abraham or to his seed through the law, but through the righteousness of faith.

What these verses reveal is that our relationship with God is established by faith in Him. We believe in Him, and by faith and obedience we give our lives to Him, recognizing God as our Savior and Lord. We are then asked by God to live in a manner that reflects His character. We are saved at the moment when we exercise faith in God, and then our task is to begin to live like who we have become: His children.

Our relationship with God is established by faith in Him.

Throughout the Old Testament, God initiates a number of covenants with His people, but the one that dominates is the Mosaic covenant. God chose the nation of Israel to be His people and He agreed to be their God. This relationship, of course, as we have already seen, had to be established on faith. The offer of God to redeem humanity is *always* based on faith alone. There is nothing that humanity can do to earn righteousness and a relationship with God.

Therefore, because of our faith, as we saw in Romans 4:2–3, God imputes righteousness to us. He accepts our faith in Him as a reason to give us His righteousness. Nevertheless, as we accept

God's covenant to be His children and have Him be our God, He
then asks us to live in a way that reflects His character and His
values. Nothing demonstrates this more completely than the Mosaic covenant, which was established on Mount Sinai when God
gave Moses the Ten Commandments to bring down to the children of Israel. However, the Mosaic Law included hundreds of
laws in addition to the Ten Commandments.

I used to think how unfair it was that God chose Israel to the
exclusion of all other peoples. Then as I began to understand
more about God's intention and the truth revealed in the Old Testament, I saw that God did not choose Israel to the exclusion of all
of the other peoples on earth, but that God chose Israel in order *to
reach* the others. We see this stated clearly in Psalm 67:1, 2, 5–7:

> God be merciful to us and bless us,
> And cause His face to shine upon us.
> Selah.
> That Your way may be known on earth,
> Your salvation among all nations.
> Let the peoples praise You, O God;
> Let all the peoples praise You.
> Then the earth shall yield her increase;
> God, our own God, shall bless us.
> God shall bless us,
> And all the ends of the earth shall fear Him.

This Psalm teaches us that God's intent is to bless a faithful
and obedient Israel to such an extent that all of the other nations
of the world will see the thumbprint of God in the nation of Israel and desire to know God because of what they see of Him in
the life of the Israelites.

The Mosaic Law is often seen as oppressive and restrictive.
Certainly it is restrictive, but it is not oppressive. Properly seen,
it was meant to show people how to live a joyous and abundant
life. The Law is a gracious gift of God that reflects His character
and offers people a motivation and lifestyle that they would
never come up with on their own. There are great requirements
within the Mosaic Law, but those great requirements yield stupendous blessing. We read in Psalm 1, for example, verses 1–3:

> Blessed is the man who walks not in the counsel of the ungodly,
> nor stands in the path of sinners, nor sits in the seat of the scornful;
> but his delight *is* in the law of the Lord, and in His law he meditates
> day and night. He shall be like a tree planted by the rivers of water,

that brings forth its fruit in its season, whose leaf also shall not wither; and whatever he does shall prosper.

We see here that if people delight in the law of the Lord, and meditate in it and (by implication) are faithfully obedient to it, then they will have fruit, health, and prosperity in their lives. Another powerful statement of the blessing of the Mosaic Law is found in Psalm 19:7–11, where we read:

> The law of the Lord *is* perfect, converting the soul; the testimony of the Lord is sure, making wise the simple; the statutes of the Lord are right, rejoicing the heart; the commandment of the Lord is pure, enlightening the eyes; the fear of the Lord is clean, enduring forever; the judgments of the Lord are true and righteous altogether. More to be desired are they than gold, yea, than much fine gold; sweeter also than honey and the honeycomb. Moreover by them Your servant is warned, and in keeping them there *is* great reward.

So we see that the Mosaic Law is indeed full of laws, testimonies, statutes, commandments and judgments, and in faithfully following these elements of the law, the soul is restored, the simple are made wise, the heart rejoices, the eyes are enlightened, and we have a great reward.

The great requirements of the Mosaic Law yield stupendous blessings.

In addition, throughout Psalm 119, David repeatedly extols the virtue and value of the laws of God and how they bring freedom, blessing, abundance, health, and hope. Following the Mosaic covenant saves God's people from the pain of living a life that violates His character.

Throughout the Old Testament a central part of God's promises to His people was that a Messiah would come to be the final solution for their sins. He would usher in a kingdom which would not have the pain, suffering, and sorrow that existed within the earthly kingdom of Israel. These promises were often a cause of intense struggle within the hearts of the faithful in Israel because they saw the righteous suffering and the unrighteous prospering. Nevertheless, passages in Psalms, Proverbs, and the Book of Job contain assurances and hopes that this will eventually be corrected. After thousands of years, however, immediately preceding the birth of Jesus, one of Israel's cries was, "Oh, Lord, how long?" meaning how long will it be before You bring peace and righteousness to Your people.

What Is Christ?

Christ is the fulfillment of God's Old Testament covenant promises for Messiah to come to redeem humanity.

Jesus came in direct fulfillment of many Old Testament promises about a Messiah who would come to redeem Israel from her sins and to establish justice and righteousness on the earth. The picture of exactly who this Messiah would be, when He would come, and what He would do was not at all clear to Old Testament saints.

For example, some Old Testament prophecies about the coming Messiah (translated "Christ" in the New Testament) indicated that He would come as a lowly servant and that He would be humble and would suffer terribly. Other prophecies indicated that the Messiah would come as a reigning King in great power and glory. Understandably Old Testament saints had a difficult time putting these two pictures of the Messiah together.

How could one person fulfill both of these pictures? It was such a difficult problem that some Old Testament people suggested that there would be two Messiahs; one Messiah who would come as a servant, be humble and lowly and suffer; the second Messiah would come as a great King reigning in power and glory. With what information they had at hand, the concept of two Messiahs was reasonable. As "the parade of history" has unfolded, however, we now have a fuller understanding, which is that there is only one Messiah who would come twice. The first time He came as a humble servant to suffer and die for our sins. This same Messiah will return to earth a second time as a great King in power and glory to reign over all the earth.

This feature of messianic prophecy and fulfillment gives us a principle for interpreting many prophecies and fulfillments in the Bible; namely, that many prophecies are fulfilled partially in the short run and ultimately only in the long run.

For example, the kingdom of God has already been inaugurated by Jesus at His first coming, and yet it has not come in its fullness and completeness. Several biblical passages suggest this. For example, in Matthew 12 some people brought Jesus a demon-possessed man who was blind and mute, and Jesus cast the demon out of him and healed him. When this man then spoke and saw, the religious leaders accused Jesus of casting demons out by using the power of Satan. Jesus' response was that a house divided against itself could not stand, that Satan would not cast out his own forces. Then Jesus says, in verse 28, "But if I cast out demons by the Spirit of God, surely the kingdom of God has come upon you." This is an irrefutable reference to the inauguration of the kingdom of God.

The apostle Paul also made it clear that the kingdom of God had dawned (Romans 14:17; 1 Corinthians 4:20; 1 Corinthians 15:24).

Many prophecies are fulfilled partially now and fully only in the long run.

But it is equally clear from other passages, such as Matthew 6:10, 1 Corinthians 6:9–10, and Ephesians 5:5, that the kingdom of God has not come in its fullness and completeness. Clearly, the day the apostle John writes about in Revelation 21:4 has not yet come: when "God will wipe away every tear from their eyes; there shall be no more death, nor sorrow, nor crying. There shall be no more pain, for the former things have passed away."

So far, then, we can summarize by saying that as the great parade of history passes by the grandstand of our observation, the first float is "creation." God created a world in perfect peace and harmony—a paradise, if you will, in which He intended environment to be sustained; in which He could love humanity and be loved by humanity in the glory and joy of full righteousness. This original creation, however, was contaminated by the entrance of sin. Humanity was separated from God because of sin and was utterly unable to correct the situation.

God, then, in His graciousness and righteousness, brings the second float by the grandstand, the "covenant," through which He initiates a plan to restore us to His original purpose and intention. As a covenant-making God, He agrees to redeem us by grace through faith in Him. In response He asks us to live a life that reflects the God who has saved us.

This time of covenant in the Old Testament centered around the coming of a Messiah who would redeem fallen humanity from its sin, inaugurate the kingdom of God, and restore faithful humanity to His original purpose and intention. However, when Jesus Christ came as the fulfillment of the Old Testament messianic promises, He inaugurated only a partial fulfillment of the Old Testament prophecies concerning the coming of the kingdom of God. Clearly, He did not fulfill the glories of the kingdom of God in their fullness. Apparently, according to a characteristic of biblical prophecy, we see a partial fulfillment of those prophecies concerning a kingdom of God being inaugurated with Jesus' first coming, and we will not see the complete fulfillment of those prophecies until Jesus returns a second time.

What Is the Church?

The church is the totality of all believers in Jesus Christ who are to carry out His will on earth until He comes again.

The next float to pass the grandstand is the "church," an entity in God's historical program that was not clearly seen in the Old Testament. After all, nearly all of Jesus' followers were astonished when He was crucified. It was an end to His ministry that none of them seemed prepared to accept.

However, three days after His crucifixion Jesus rose from the dead and revealed Himself to His followers, and the seed of hope for the future of the gospel began to germinate in the hearts of His closest disciples (Matthew 20:1–20). Later, after many other meetings with them, He talked with them on the Mount of Olives, where He gave them their final instructions before His departure from the earth. We read in Acts 1:8–9:

> But you shall receive power when the Holy Spirit has come upon you; and you shall be witnesses to Me in Jerusalem, and in all Judea and Samaria, and to the end of the earth. Now when He had spoken these things, while they watched, He was taken up, and a cloud received Him out of their sight.

This is an astonishing event no matter how you look at it. To have Jesus rise up off the ground and disappear into a cloud is amazing enough. But this event is then followed shortly afterward by the descent of the Holy Spirit to earth in a way that had never been seen before: each believer in Jesus became indwelt by the Holy Spirit and the entity known as the church began.

The church's task today is the same as when Jesus walked on earth.

The church is called the "body of Christ" in the New Testament. And the task of the church is the same as the task Jesus had while He was on the earth; namely, manifesting the character of God and proclaiming the message of salvation by grace through faith in Jesus Christ. This great charge is now transferred to the church as it functions in Christ's place as His collective body. The church has a number of distinctions that characterize it.

- Each person who is a genuine believer in Jesus Christ is born again and is given the Holy Spirit as a seal that guarantees his or her inheritance until the redemption of the purchased possession (Ephesians 1:13, 14).

- Each individual is given a spiritual gift that is a supernatural capacity to have a spiritual ministry in the lives of other people (1 Peter 4:10).

- Each Christian is given a commission by Christ to participate in the evangelization of the world. In Matthew 28:19–20, we see what is commonly referred to as the Great Commission when Jesus said:

  Go therefore and make disciples of all the nations, baptizing them in the name of the Father and of the Son and of the Holy Spirit, teaching them to observe all things that I have commanded you; and lo, I am with you always, even to the end of the age.

- This commission is passed down by implication to all His disciples, each of whom must make the decision to accept the Great Commission to evangelize the world as part of his own personal responsibility to God.

- Each person is given a commission to do what he can to help build the church. Jesus said in Matthew 16:18, ". . . I will build My church, and the gates of Hades shall not prevail against it." Then in the fourth chapter of Ephesians, all Christians are charged to do their part to maintain the spiritual unity of the church, to exercise their spiritual gifts for the purpose of the church, and, in general, to contribute to the lives of other Christians in such a way that they all grow up to maturity in Jesus Christ.

- Christians are given the commission to help make the world a better place in which to live. The apostle Paul wrote in Galatians 6:10, "Therefore, as we have opportunity, let us do good to all, especially to those who are of the household of faith." This suggests that Christians have the task of doing good in the world.

- We are given the responsibility to worship the Lord and to observe baptism and the Lord's Supper and to maintain a ready spirit until Jesus comes again in the complete fulfillment of God's covenant promises.

What Is the Consummation?

Consummation is the completion of God's redemptive plan.

The fifth and final float in our parade is "consummation," or the end of the age. When we see all of history as one parade passing by the grandstand, we can better envision that the future is merely the will of God already determined, but which has yet to occur. Therefore, we need not have concerns about the future or worries that things are not going to work out the way they should. The will of God has already decreed that they shall. Properly seen, prophecy is just the culmination of the plan which God established before creation. It is merely the last float in the parade, all of which is seen by God.

God created humanity for friendship and fellowship with Him. When that original plan was destroyed through the Fall, God instituted His recovery plan of redemption in four remaining stages: covenant, Christ, church, and, ultimately, consummation. We are somewhere in that fourth stage, the church. And the consummation is yet to be realized. Nevertheless, in order to be accurately seen, it must be seen as an already accomplished fact in the mind of God, a "float" that has already been created but which has yet to pass the grandstand.

In God's mind, the consummation of all this is an accomplished fact.

Several important points can be made about the consummation period.

- First, we do not know when the consummation of history will occur. The nature of prophecy concerning the consummation period is such that the consummation period could occur at any moment and yet it could be delayed for an undetermined length of time.

- The second point about Christ's return is that it spurred the early church to be heavily involved in evangelism. This emphasis on evangelism came from two places, I believe. First, it was motivated by the compassion the early church had for all who need to experience salvation by grace through faith in Jesus Christ, Second, it came from Matthew 24:14, which suggests that the return of Christ would not occur until the gospel was first preached to all nations. Therefore, the church that is eagerly looking forward to the return of Christ would also be committed to evangelism as a prerequisite to that return.

• Third, because the return of Christ could happen in any generation, the early church took seriously the call to a holy lifestyle. It is the call of every Christian in every generation to live in the present evil age while embracing the values of the age to come. They must live like citizens of heaven while they are citizens of earth (Titus 2:11–14).

• Fourth, because Christ could return in any generation, the early church had a high respect for the value of suffering. These believers knew that suffering in this age would have its counterpart in glory in the age to come. The more suffering one experienced in this life, the more glory one could expect in the next. This conviction helped those early Christians to be much less afraid of suffering, for they had a much stronger grip on the values of eternity than on the values of this world.

• Fifth, because Jesus could return in any age, the early church should be dedicated to the task of spiritual warfare. The early church recognized that much of the struggle of the present life was rooted in the great cosmic battle between God and His forces and Satan and his forces. The apostle Paul wrote in Colossians 2:15 that, "Having disarmed principalities and powers, He made a public spectacle of them, triumphing over them in it." This passage makes it clear that the battle is won and yet other passages such as Ephesians 6:10–13 indicate that the battle, though the outcome is assured, can nevertheless rage hot and heavy at any given moment until Jesus does return.

In summary, we can say with all the assurance of the Scriptures that while we cannot know the *exact* time of Christ's return, we must live as if it *could* happen at any moment. It is this message that empowers Christians to live with the implications of the Second Coming every day of their lives. At the same time, while living in light of that fact that the consummation of history could be at hand, we must realize that Jesus might *not* come in our generation or even possibly for another 2000 years. And in that case, we need to plan responsibly for the future and try to do all within our power and the leading of God to help establish kingdom principles in the midst of an ungodly world.

Conclusion

We have already alluded to the following in our illustration of the parade floats of history, but additional emphasis will strengthen the concept in our minds. In a way that we cannot fully understand, God exists outside of time. He existed before time as we know it began. And He will exist after time as we know it comes to an end. Everything that occurs within the confines of time as we know it from the creation of the world until the end of this world is known to God—past, present, and future. Because God is omniscient (all-knowing), He knows all things both actual and possible. Because He is omnipotent (all-powerful), He is able to do whatever He chooses to do, and God has chosen from before the beginning of creation to establish a world in which His highest creation, humanity, could worship Him, fellowship with Him, and rule and reign with Him over creation for eternity. Since the plan is His, and since He has the power to execute His plan, the things of the future are just as certain as the things of the past. Therefore, God is fully able to make known to humanity that which is going to happen in the future. In fact, because God is sovereign over creation and can direct the course of history, future events are merely the culmination of what God started with original creation.

Speed Bump!
Slow down to be sure you've gotten the main points of this chapter.

Question
Answer

Q1. What is creation?

A1. Creation is the *beginning* of the universe and human life.

Q2. What is covenant?

A2. A covenant is a binding *agreement* between two individuals, and God has embarked on a series of agreements with humanity.

Q3. What is Christ?

A3. Christ is the *fulfillment* of God's Old Testament covenant promises for Messiah to come to redeem humanity.

Q4. What is the church?

A4. The church is the totality of all *believers* in Jesus Christ who are to carry out His will on earth until He comes again.

Q5. What is the consummation?

A5. Consummation is the *completion* of God's redemptive plan.

Fill in the Blanks

Q**uestion**
A**nswer**

Q1. What is creation?

A1. Creation is the _____ of the universe and human life.

Q2. What is covenant?

A2. A covenant is a binding _____ between two individuals, and God has embarked on a series of agreements with humanity.

Q3. What is Christ?

A3. Christ is the _____ of God's Old Testament covenant promises for Messiah to come to redeem humanity.

Q4. What is the church?

A4. The church is the totality of all _____ in Jesus Christ who are to carry out His will on earth until He comes again.

Q5. What is the consummation?

A5. Consummation is the _____ of God's redemptive plan.

For Further Thought and Discussion

1. What events that happen to you, or to those around you, make it hardest for you to believe that God is in control?

2. How does the illustration of the parade floats help you to deal with those hard things?

3. How does the concept of God's covenants with us encourage you to believe that the consummation will happen as predicted?

What If I Don't Believe?

If I don't believe in God's big plan for humanity, I am very likely to become quite discouraged about the deep problems the world is in. It would be easy for me to lose confidence that God is in control; it would be easy to think that everything is happening at random. I am liable to lose the peace that comes from knowing that God is in control, even though world events and personal events may not seem like it.

For Further Study

1. Scripture

- Genesis 1–2
- Romans 4:2–3
- Romans 4:13
- Psalm 67:1–7
- Psalm 1
- Psalm 19:7–11
- Mark 1:14–15
- Luke 17:20–21
- Romans 14:17; 1 Corinthians 6:9–10
- Matthew 28:19–20
- Titus 2:11–14

2. Books
Other books helpful in studying this subject are:

God Has Spoken, James Packer
Doomsday Delusions, C. Marvin Pate and Calvin B. Haines, Jr.

It's taken me all my life to understand that it is not
necessary to understand everything.
■ René-Jules-Gustave Coty (1882–1962)

How Do We Explain Differences of Understanding in Prophecy?

Shortly after my seminary education a striking thing happened to me that deeply affected my view of prophecy. The seminary that I graduated from took a literal view toward the fulfillment of most biblical prophecies. And, as you might expect, so did I. Shortly after I graduated, a highly respected professor, who had taught at the seminary during the time I attended, left the seminary and began a personal inward journey, and the result was that he adopted a view of prophecy which was more figurative.

This intrigued me greatly, and in the providence of God I had a couple of opportunities to talk with him about his journey from a more literal to a more figurative view of prophecy. Those conversations, plus a number of conversations with other key people, as well as my own reading and thinking, brought me to a point of high tolerance for responsible differences of opinion on the subject.

In this chapter we learn that . . .

1. Interpretation varies, and some prophecies should be understood literally while others should be understood symbolically.
2. Some prophecies had both an immediate and a future fulfillment.
3. Factors such as upbringing, education, and temperament influence interpretation of prophecies.
4. We should read prophecy in its historical, grammatical, and literary context, relying on the whole context of Scripture.

While I still hold to the view of Bible prophecy that I had when I graduated from seminary, I now have a high respect for many people who hold to a different opinion. And much of this is due to my observations and discussions regarding the prophetic odyssey of the above professor. For example, he had two doctorates, one from the seminary and one from an Ivy League school, so I could not fault him for having a weak education or for being unintelligent. He was also more spiritually mature than I was, so I could not fault him for spiritual immaturity. He was generally regarded on campus as one of the most deeply spiritual men in the seminary, so much so that it was often remarked by the students that it was a privilege simply to listen to his prayers, which he said each day before class.

If I could not fault him for a weak education, or for a weak mind, or for spiritual immaturity, then on what basis could I fault him for his conversion from a more literal to a more figurative interpretation of Bible prophecy? I concluded that I could not fault him on any grounds, even though I had not been persuaded by his experience to make the same theological revision.

This puzzled me and I began thinking seriously over the next decade about what causes a person to hold to one or the other of the major views of biblical prophecy. I looked outside the experiences of my seminary professor and myself to many of the great ministers of our day. I have accumulated books written by giants of the faith, godly, gifted, and blessed men who minister with the obvious anointing of God. As a result, I can line up giants on the side of the more literal interpretation and I can line up an equal number on the side of the more figurative interpretation. And, by the quality of their education, by the quality of their intellect, and by the quality of their spiritual lives, I cannot say that one side is superior to the other on any of those grounds.

Why I need to know this

If I don't understand the valid uncertainties of interpreting prophetic Scripture, I may make one of two mistakes: I may think that I am right and everybody else is wrong, or I may think that it is impossible to understand anything at all about prophetic Scripture. Both extremes are errors.

This helped me to conclude that a person's fundamental view of biblical prophecy probably had something to do with matters in addition to education, intellect, and spirituality. That in itself was a dramatic revelation to me, and it strengthened my determination to hold the people in both camps with deep respect. But it also set me on a search to try to account for why the differences exist in spite of education, intellect, and spiritual maturity.

It is those issues that I want to address in this chapter, for the purpose of helping us all to have a broader, deeper understanding of biblical prophecy as well as a greater respect for those who might hold to a position different from our own. In his poem, *The Everlasting Gospel*, William Blake wrote, "The vision of Christ that thou doest see / is my vision's greatest enemy." "And both read the Bible day and night, / But thou read'st black where I read white." It is this phenomenon that we want to explore to see how it relates to the issue of biblical prophecy.

Are Prophecies to Be Understood Literally or Symbolically?

Interpretation varies, and some prophecies should be understood literally while others should be understood symbolically.

There are many examples, particularly in the Old Testament, where a prophet predicted specific events in clear language, and it seems obvious that the prophecy is intended to have a literal fulfillment in history. For example, in the Book of Isaiah, chapters 44:24–45:13, Isaiah proclaims that God is going to raise up a man named Cyrus who is going to permit Jews to return to Jerusalem and rebuild it. We know from history that 150 years later Cyrus became king of Persia and permitted the Jews, who were in captivity in Babylonia, to return to Jerusalem and rebuild the city's walls and the temple and to reestablish sacrificial worship to their God. To all but the most skeptical, this is a clear prophecy—history written in advance—which was fulfilled specifically and literally.

Other prophetic passages in the Bible cannot be taken literally and are clearly intended to be taken figuratively. One example is found in Revelation 6:13, where we read, "and the stars of the sky fell to the earth." We know that stars are many times larger than the earth and that it would be impossible for them to fall to the earth without obliterating the earth many times over before they ever got close to it.

> In biblical prophecy, a literal meaning is behind a symbolic picture.

There is a literal meaning behind the symbolic picture; nevertheless, the actual wording was not intended to be taken literally. But whenever we have prophetic language that is clearly figurative, it always opens the door for multiple possible interpretations.

It is not at all uncommon for us to use symbolic, or figurative, language; for example, when we say one thing and mean
another. In the well-known hymn "Amazing Grace," the first
stanza reads, "Amazing grace, how sweet the sound that saved a
wretch like me. I once was lost, but now am found, was blind,
but now I see." We know that John Newton was not physically,
literally, blind when he wrote that, nor was he ever blind during
his lifetime. When he said he was blind, he meant it spiritually;
he meant that he did not see the truth of God and the need to
live one's life in dedication to Jesus. He meant that he did not
understand the spiritual truth that guides the Christian life. He
meant symbolically and figuratively that he was blind. However,
if a non-Christian, non-English-speaking person got a translated
copy of that stanza and did not understand the context, he might
easily think that Newton was at one time physically blind but
had somehow gained eyesight.

Those of us who understand the context of the hymn and
who know the history of John Newton find it quite easy to understand what Newton was saying in his hymn. But take away
an understanding of context, and take away an understanding of
the writer's history, and understanding his hymn would not be
easy. The same is true of prophetic Scripture.

Does Each Prophecy Refer to Only One Event in History?

Some prophecies had both an immediate and a future fulfillment.

In Isaiah 7, the Lord prophesies through Isaiah to King Ahaz
to provide critical information concerning the welfare of the nation of Judah. Some kings from the north were coming to destroy
Jerusalem, and the Lord spoke to Ahaz through Isaiah telling
him that these nations would not be successful in destroying the
city. Furthermore, those very kings would soon be destroyed.

In confirmation, the Lord instructs Isaiah to tell King Ahaz,
beginning in verse 14, "Therefore the Lord Himself will give you
a sign: Behold, the virgin shall conceive and bear a Son, and shall
call His name Immanuel. Curds and honey He shall eat, that He
may know to refuse the evil and choose the good. For before the
Child shall know to refuse the evil and choose the good, the land
that you dread will be forsaken by both her kings."

Apparently this verse had an immediate application to the king of Judah: a woman as yet unmarried at the time of the prophecy would marry and have a baby boy, and while this boy was still young the nations that wanted to destroy Jerusalem would themselves be destroyed.

Centuries later, however, the Holy Spirit led the apostle Matthew to quote Isaiah 7:14 as a prophecy that would also be true of a virgin birth, specifically the birth of a child to a woman who was still a virgin. This was the first of many prophecies about the Messiah given by Isaiah, and in this prophecy we see both an immediate application to Ahaz and the nation of Judah and a future application to Mary and Joseph (Matthew 1:22–23).

Opinions concerning Isaiah's prophecy may differ because the prophet did not indicate and may not have realized that his prophecy had both an immediate and a future application. Furthermore, not all of the examples of this kind of prophecy are as clear as Isaiah 7:14, since Matthew refers to it specifically. That prophecy clearly refers to Jesus and His miraculous conception by the Holy Spirit.

Another problem that deserves a quick mention here is that it is difficult to know whether to take some prophetic passages literally or figuratively. In such passages, it is not easy to discover whether they are about historical, literal events or not, or even whether those events have occurred or will occur literally.

What Personal Factors Might Influence Different Interpretations of Prophecy?

Factors such as upbringing, education, and temperament can influence interpretation of prophecies.

Everything that we have said up to this point reveals that prophetic writings often give rise to more than one viable interpretation. Further, in some cases we may not be able to know what is the intended interpretation of the prophecy.

Furthermore, I believe that additional personal factors also account for some of the differences of interpretation of prophecy.

One major factor is a person's upbringing. For example, if a child is reared in a Christian home which takes a literal view of prophecy, that child will learn a great deal about literal prophetic interpretation and probably little about symbolic or figurative interpretation. The child therefore grows up not knowing that more than one interpretation is possible.

Closely related to the example of parental upbringing is the person who does not grow up in a Christian home but who becomes a Christian under the influence of a local church. Commonly, that person then learns his first biblical truth under the teaching of that local church and frequently ends up embracing its prophetic perspective. This isn't wrong, it's just the normal way things happen.

External sources and personal tendencies influence different interpretations of prophecy.

Education is also a significant influence on one's interpretation of prophetic Scripture. Regardless of whether or not a person grows up in a Christian home or has been well instructed in a local church, when he gets to a Christian college or a seminary, that educational institution will greatly influence how he interprets prophetic Scripture. For example, a Christian who attends a Presbyterian seminary will likely graduate with a different prophetic perspective than if he attends a conservative Baptist seminary.

The reason for this is, of course, that we are influenced, and properly so, by those people who teach us the Bible. Furthermore, if a person grew up in a home where a literal interpretation of prophecy was embraced, and if that person also went to a church and a seminary that reinforced that view, then it is probable that that person will live and die with a literal interpretation of prophetic Scripture. Of course, this type of conditioning regarding prophetic interpretation would also be true for anyone growing up and having a figurative view reinforced throughout life.

Our upbringing, then, as well as the education we receive from respected Christian leaders, has a strong influence on our interpretation of Scripture.

In addition, I believe there is an internal factor that greatly influences a person's prophetic perspective. And it often explains why a person may end up with a different perspective than that of his family, his church, or even the theological institution where he was trained. This has to do with personal temperament. I mentioned this topic in another book in this series, *What You Need to Know about The Bible:*

> It seems to me that humanity can be classified into one of two large categories. I'm not sure what labels you give the categories, but

one kind of person tends to take Scripture figuratively and the other, quite literally. One person is flexible, tolerant, and open-minded. The other is staunch, protective, and cautious. The one tends to see gray. The other tends to see black and white.

I couldn't prove this if my life depended on it, but I believe that people are inclined this way from birth, and that it affects everything in their life, from political philosophy through social issues and to morality and beyond. I don't believe one (tendency) is right and the other wrong. Both can have their own great strengths and terrible weaknesses. The staunch person may defend the faith very well, while the tolerant person lets a crucial doctrine erode. On the other hand, the staunch person may spend his time fighting other Christians over things that don't really matter, when he should be using his time and energy to advance the cause of Christ among non-Christians. The tolerant person may be winning more people to Christ in one year than the staunch person does in his entire lifetime. The key, it seems to me, is to recognize and understand your own nature, capitalize on your strengths, and try to avoid your weaknesses (147).

Does this mean that there are no valid differences of opinion concerning prophecy? Does it mean that our prophetic interpretation of a given passage is a consequence of factors beyond our control? I don't believe that is the case.

In many cases, differences of interpretation arise simply because some people do not understand how to interpret Scripture. The principles used to interpret the Bible are the same as those used to interpret the U.S. Constitution or the writings of Julius Caesar or Benjamin Franklin. If we disregard those principles, we will misconstrue the meaning of those writings. So even in the light of our natural tendency to interpret things differently and to come under the influence of external sources, we can nevertheless minimize faulty interpretation of prophecy by knowing the principles of interpretation.

How Should We Read and Attempt to Understand Prophecy?

We should read prophecy in its historical, grammatical, and literary context relying on the whole context of Scripture.

Besides all the above reasons, prophetic Scripture may be hard to interpret for even more reasons, such as the passing of time. The books of the Bible were composed over a 1500-year period that ended almost 2000 years ago. The world has changed a great deal since those words were written. Our modern cultures are vastly different than those biblical times. So much time has passed that things which were perfectly obvious to a person

Clear principles of interpretation are essential for understanding biblical prophecy.

when the Bible was written can be incomprehensible to us today.

But all is not lost. Helpful principles enable us to be successful at interpreting prophetic literature, even though some biblical prophecies may remain a mystery to us.

We said, however, that we should read prophecy in its historical, grammatical, and literary context. With that in mind, we will now look at these three helpful principles and guidelines.

Historical Background

All biblical prophecies were written in a specific time and place, by a specific person, and for a specific people. If we are going to comprehend the prophetic literature, we need to know as much as possible about the historical background of a prophecy. For example, in Revelation 3:14–22, Christ condemns the church of Laodicea for being "neither cold nor hot." He then says, "I could wish you were either cold or hot." In their book *Introduction to Biblical Interpretation*, William Klein and Craig Bomberg write:

> We must interpret "hot" and "cold" in light of the historical context of Laodicea, which was located close to both a hot spring (by Hierapolis) and a cold stream (by Colossae). Now both hot and cold water are desirable; both are useful for distinct purposes. But the spiritual state of this church more closely resembled the tepid lukewarm water that eventually flowed into Laodicean pipes; neither hot nor cold, it was putrid and emetic (causing vomiting). Jesus is *not* saying that active opposition to Him (an incorrect interpretation of "cold") is better than being a lukewarm Christian (175–176).

As we try to understand the historical context of a book, there are a number of things we can do (adapted from A. Berkeley Mickelson, *Interpreting the Bible*):

- Know the peoples who are involved in the passage being interpreted.

- Determine what time period is likely.

- Check where the place is on a map.

- Note the customs, the material objects of the culture, the social and religious relationships that are in the story.

- Recognize how the history of the place and the times influenced the responses and attitudes of the original hearers or readers.

- Note not just the similarities but the differences between the Biblical culture of the story and the surrounding pagan influences, history, and culture.

- Note both similarities or differences in matters of measurement and language between today's technical-scientific world and Biblical culture.

- Be aware of both similarities and differences between the historical-cultural setting of the original writer and reader and your own historical-cultural situation (176).

In doing this, the use of a good Bible handbook can be extremely helpful. You can find one at any well-stocked Christian bookstore, and it will usually provide all of the information just mentioned.

Meanings of Words

Most words express more than one meaning. For example, the English word "trunk" might refer to the trunk of a tree, or a large piece of luggage, or an elephant's nose, or a human's torso, or the back compartment of an automobile. When we say the word *trunk,* we have to depend on the context of the word and the surrounding grammar in order to know what is meant by the word in a particular place.

The original Hebrew and Greek can convey subtle meanings necessary for understanding prophecy.

This fact also applies to the words we read in Scripture. For example, the word that the King James Version translates several times as "conversation" does not refer to talking, as it does today. It meant "a manner of life," or "conduct." So, curiously, we must not take even the English words of the Bible for granted. We must discover what they refer to, which may be something quite different than what we think. One of the surest ways of accomplishing this is to compare how different versions of the Bible translate a given original word.

The biblical languages of Hebrew for the Old Testament and Greek for the New Testament sometimes convey subtle meanings that cannot be translated easily into English. For this reason, it is helpful to consult a good Bible commentary after studying the passage. This helps to determine whether or not your interpretation of the passage has been understood.

Literary Context

The Bible contains a number of different kinds, or forms, of writing. These all have their own rules of interpretation, which are covered in another volume in this series titled *What You Need to Know about the Bible*. In that volume, the literary form that we are focusing on in this volume, prophecy, was also discussed:

> Interpreting prophetic literature can be extremely difficult because so much symbolic, figurative, and non-literal material fills it, and we are not always told what the literal reality is behind the figurative language. A few guidelines, however, help greatly.
>
> First, as with any passage in the Bible, study its history, context, and literal meaning. Study the historical circumstances of both the prophet and the people to whom he prophesied. Carefully consider both the immediate and broad contexts. Take the words in their normal sense unless a figure of speech or a symbol is evidently being used, or unless the passage just doesn't make sense when taken literally. For example, Revelation talks of stars falling to the earth, and stars could not fall to the earth without obliterating it. So the stars must mean something other than literal stars.
>
> Next, identify to whom the passage is written or what the passage is talking about. Is the passage forthtelling or foretelling? Has the prophecy been fulfilled? If it has been, study the writings that tell about the fulfillment. Is it still unfulfilled? If so, study it carefully and humbly. Unfulfilled prophecy is often very mysterious because of its use of symbolism. Since prophecy is so difficult, prophecy teachers can be helpful, but they can also be confusing since not all teachers agree on what symbolic language means. Different "schools" of opinion bring various perspectives to Bible prophecy, and it can be challenging but rewarding to become educated in this area.
>
> Finally, remember that the main purpose of prophecy is not to inspire debate, tickle our curiosity or fuel our opinions. Rather, its purpose is to encourage faith in God and to encourage holy living. For example, Paul introduces his discussion of the future (1 Thessalo-

nians 4:13–18) by saying that he did not want the Thessalonian be- lievers to be ignorant or to grieve as those who have no hope. In con- trast to false teachers who evidently were teaching that their loved ones who died before Christ's return would not be raised to new life, Paul proclaimed that "the dead in Christ will rise first" (v. 16), and all believers "shall always be with the Lord. Therefore comfort one an- other with these words" (v. 17–18).

God desires the promise of Christ's return to have a motivating and purifying effect on the personal life and ministry of Christians (see Titus 2:11–14), and not for its timing to become a source of con- flict and division. Therefore, when you study biblical prophecy, al- ways ask yourself, "How does God intend this truth to change my life?" (161–162).

A point that needs to be emphasized is that the literary con- text should emphasize the use of the whole of Scripture to understand a particular passage, **Use the whole** rather than lifting out verses and inadvertently **context of Scripture** using them out of context to support a given, **to interpret** and perhaps an erroneous, interpretation. In **prophecy.** many cases a passage from another part of Scripture best inter- prets what a given prophecy elsewhere in Scripture might mean. We must be sure to interpret obscure or symbolic passages in light of other clear and literal passages if they exist.

Conclusion

Even the finest biblical scholar using the most reliable princi- ples of interpretation will find many passages of prophecy that remain uncertain and unclear. There are several reasons for this.

First, we bring our own assumptions and expectations to any given interpretation of Scripture and therefore we can skew the interpretation without realizing it.

Second, there is the great gap of time, culture, and language. Some things in the Bible that were perfectly clear to those to whom it was written are unclear to us 2000 or 3000 years later.

Third, it is entirely possible that we will never understand some passages of Scripture because to us their language will re- main obscure.

And finally, we must recognize that while there are advan- tages to written communication, there are also some disadvantages; that is, spoken language is usually accompanied by facial expressions, vocal expressions, and body language. When we do not have these clues to interpret the meaning of what is spoken, we may not understand the written word. The very nature of language is ambiguous.

It is not particularly frustrating to me when I read things in the Bible that I don't understand, because I can remember that I have occasionally read things that I *myself* have written and now do not understand what I meant by them. We must recognize that interpreting prophetic literature is not a technical and precise undertaking. When trying to master prophetic literature as best we can, we must rely on an attitude of openness and obedience to what the Lord is saying. We must also rely on sound principles of interpretation bolstered by a sense of peace, realizing that we will not understand all prophecies. Through all of this, the Holy Spirit will make sure that we understand all of the Bible that we need to in order to be able to walk in God's will. Finally, we must respect those who hold to responsible opposing positions.

Speed Bump!

Slow down to be sure you've gotten the main points of this chapter.

Question

Answer

Q1. Are prophecies to be understood literally or symbolically?

A1. Interpretation *varies,* and some prophecies should be understood literally while others should be understood symbolically.

Q2. Does each prophecy refer to only one event in history?

A2. Some prophecies had both an immediate and a *future* fulfillment.

Q3. What personal factors might influence different interpretations of prophecy?

A3. Factors such as upbringing, education, and *temperament* influence interpretation of prophecies.

Q4. How should we read and attempt to understand prophecy?

A4. We should read prophecy in its historical, grammatical, and literary *context,* relying on the whole context of Scripture.

Fill in the Blank

Question   **Q1.** Are prophecies to be understood literally or symbolically?

Answer   **A1.** Interpretation _____ , and some prophecies should be understood literally while others should be understood symbolically.

Q2. Does each prophecy refer to only one event in history?

A2. Some prophecies had both an immediate and a _____ fulfillment.

Q3. What personal factors might influence different interpretations of prophecy?

A3. Factors such as upbringing, education, and _____ influence interpretation of prophecies.

Q4. How should we read and attempt to understand prophecy?

A4. We should read prophecy in its historical, grammatical, and literary _____ relying on the whole context of Scripture.

For Further Thought and Discussion

1. Do you think your temperament tends to see things black and white, or more in shades of gray?

2. How do you think your temperament has influenced your tendency to understand the Bible?

3. What other background factors do you think have affected your approach to understanding the Bible?

4. What strengths and weaknesses do you think you bring to understanding the Bible?

What If I Don't Believe?

If I don't believe that prophecy is a difficult, inexact subject to interpret, then I may develop a tendency to become too dogmatic in my own interpretation of Scripture, not allowing adequate possibilities for responsible differences of interpretation. Also, I may fail to give adequate respect to brothers and sisters in Christ because I have too great a confidence in my own opinions.

On the other hand, if I don't believe that there are some rules and guidelines for interpreting prophecy, which allow me to develop some reasonable confidence in my understanding of it, then I may feel overwhelmed by the task and neglect a proper study of the subject.

For Further Study

1. Scripture

Two key passages help us establish our perspective on Scripture and prophecy. They are:

- 2 Timothy 3:16–17

- 2 Peter 1:19–21

2. Books

There are two helpful books which contribute to a good base for prophetic interpretation. They are:

Doomsday Delusion, C. Marvin Pate and Calvin B. Haines, Jr.
The Last Days Handbook, Robert Lightner

When all else is lost, the future still remains.
■ **Christian Bovee (1820–1904)**

4

What Are Some Key Terms Regarding "Future Things"?

The Pirates of Penzance, an operetta written by Gilbert and Sullivan, is a hilarious and dizzy farce about a ship of pirates who have trouble making a living because of the weak spot they have in their hearts for orphans, since they were all orphans. They will not attack a ship on which any of the sailors are orphans. The word gets out, and whenever the pirates of Penzance prepare to plunder another ship, that ship then claims to be comprised of orphan-sailors, so the pirates of Penzance leave them alone. As a result, they have not plundered another ship in a long time.

One of the central characters is a young man who was accidentally apprenticed as a child to the pirate ship until his twenty-first birthday. He turns twenty-one as the play opens and declares (though he loves the pirates dearly) his intent to leave the ship and, because of his English sense of honor and duty, to rid the seas of piracy. The story is a riotous recounting of the pirates' attempt to trick him into becoming a pirate again.

The point of the play that concerns us is how the child was apprenticed. He was the son of a gentleman, and as he approached his teenage years, his father told the governess to have his son apprenticed "as a ship's pilot." Being hard of hearing, the governess thought that the father said "pirate" instead of "pilot." What follows is rollicking great fun for the audience, but it also reveals a more serious issue, which is the importance of being clear about terms. The governess set in motion a series of calamitous, even if hilarious, circumstances. In real life, if we are not clear about terms when discussing biblical prophecy and future things, the results can also be calamitous, and not at all hilarious. I once read of an elderly couple who were convinced the Lord was going to return on a certain date, so they liqui-

---

In this chapter we learn that . . .

1. The Second Coming is the return of Christ to the earth at an unknown time in the future.
2. The Rapture is the sudden departure of all Christians to meet Christ in the air.
3. The Millennium refers to a period of time when Christ reigns in righteousness.
4. The Great Tribulation is a period of intense, unprecedented suffering.
5. The Antichrist embodies evil and is the key agent of Satan's resistance to the plan of God in the last days.
6. The judgment seat of Christ is the place where all Christians will receive their reward for the quality of their lives on earth.
7. The Great White Throne judgment is the place where all who have rejected God will receive the punishment for their unbelief and their life on earth.
8. Heaven and hell are the ultimate destinations of all people, depending on whether or not they truly believe in God.

---

dated all their assets, gave the money to evangelistic ministries, and had their pets put to sleep the day before the supposed return. Imagine their disappointment when it did not happen!

There are a number of key words which we must be clear about if misunderstandings are to be kept to a minimum. In this chapter, we will survey a number of the key words. In later chapters, we will examine several in depth.

What Is the Second Coming?

The Second Coming is the return of Christ to the earth at an unknown time in the future.

All Bible-believing Christians believe in the second coming of Jesus Christ. It is one of the fundamentals of the faith: Jesus *is* returning. This is a central theme throughout the New Testament. For example, in Acts 1, Jesus met with His disciples after His resurrection and instructed them not to leave Jerusalem but to wait until they were baptized with the Holy Spirit. Then in verses 9–11, we read:

> Now when He had spoken these things, while they watched, He was taken up, and a cloud received Him out of their sight. And while

---

Why I need to know this

I need to know the terms used for prophesied events so that I will not be left in the dark when I see the terms in the Bible or in other places.

---

they looked steadfastly toward heaven as He went up, behold, two men stood by them in white apparel, who also said, "Men of Galilee, why do you stand gazing up into heaven? This same Jesus, who was taken up from you into heaven, will so come in like manner as you saw Him go into heaven" (Acts 1:9–11).

This, of course, was not the first time the disciples had heard this. Jesus spoke of His return in Matthew 24 and 25. In John 14:2–3, Jesus promised that He was going away to prepare a place for His followers and that one day He would return to get them, so that they could be with Him where He was. The apostle Paul referred repeatedly to the second coming of Christ, such as in 1 Thessalonians 3:12–13, "And may the Lord make you increase and abound in love to one another and to all, just as we do to you, so that He may establish your hearts blameless in holiness before our God and Father at the coming of our Lord Jesus Christ with all His saints."

In the last chapter of the Bible, Revelation 22, we read repeatedly of Jesus' second coming. Jesus Himself said in verse 7, "Behold, I am coming quickly! Blessed is he who keeps the words of the prophecy of this book." In verse

> **The second coming of Jesus Christ is prophesied throughout the New Testament.**

12, He says, "And behold, I am coming quickly, and My reward is with Me, to give to every one according to his work." In verse 20, we read, "The one who has spoken these things says, 'I am coming soon!' So, Lord Jesus, please come soon!" (*Contemporary English Version*)

So the theme of the second coming of Christ is reiterated from Matthew to Revelation. Some Bible teachers refer to this as the "return of the Lord." This is an ambiguous phrase, which means that it must be understood in light of context in which it appears. Sometimes, a writer will use the phrase to refer to the Rapture, and sometimes he will use it to refer to the Second Coming. Context will usually make it clear what the writer meant.

What Is the Rapture?

The Rapture is the sudden departure of all Christians to meet Christ in the air.

While fundamental and evangelical Christians agree on the second coming of Christ, there are various opinions about the Rapture. Some believe that the Rapture is distinct from the Second Coming; others believe that the Rapture and the second coming of Christ are either essentially the same thing or will occur essentially simultaneously.

The term rapture does not occur in the Bible; it comes from the Latin word *rapio* which means "caught up." First Thessalonians 4:15–17 is the main passage used to teach the Rapture:

> For this we say to you by the word of the Lord, that we who are alive and remain until the coming of the Lord will by no means precede those who are asleep. For the Lord Himself will descend from heaven with a shout, with the voice of an archangel, and with the trumpet of God. And the dead in Christ will rise first. Then we who are alive and remain shall be caught up together with them in the clouds to meet the Lord in the air. And thus we shall always be with the Lord.

The primary distinction for those who believe the Rapture occurs before the Second Coming is that in the Rapture, Jesus is seen above the earth and His feet do not come down and touch it. He is there to take all Christians on earth up to meet Him in the air. Then sometime after the Rapture, Jesus returns to earth— the Second Coming; apparently at the Mount of Olives (Acts 1:11)—and remains on it to inaugurate the final events of the end times.

The Bible does not prophesy exactly when Jesus will return.

However, people who hold this view, that the Rapture and the Second Coming are distinct events, are not all united as to when the Rapture will occur. They hold three major views concerning its exact timing, which we will examine closely later.

At this time we just want to identify the terms so that they will not seem foreign later. The "Second Coming of Christ" means that Jesus is going to return to earth at some future time, though we do not know when. Interestingly, neither Jesus nor the angels know the time; only the Father in heaven knows it

(Matthew 24:36; Acts 1:7). Further, no prophecy in the Old or New Testament provides a date for the return of Christ, though signs are indicated, particularly in Matthew 24 and 25. The purpose of the Second Coming is for Jesus Christ to establish, in the fullest sense of the word, the kingdom of God forever. All the redeemed throughout all the ages will begin living with Him in righteous, unending fellowship.

What Is the Millennium?

The Millennium refers to a period of time in which Christ reigns in righteousness.

The word "millennium" comes from the Latin word meaning "one thousand." It refers to a doctrine taken from Revelation 20:1–6, in which the apostle John describes a thousand-year period when the devil is bound and thrown into a bottomless pit. With Satan and his hosts now removed, Christians reign with Christ during the Millennium. This will be a time when humanity's longing for peace, freedom, prosperity, and righteousness on earth will be realized.

There are two primary views of the Millennium. One is of Christ's literal one-thousand-year reign of righteousness on earth, in specific fulfillment of Old Testament prophecies. Other fine biblical scholars, however, understand it to be figurative or symbolic, largely in terms of Christ's righteous reign in the hearts of those who follow Him here on earth. A variation of this is that the Millennium is symbolic of the righteous reign of Christ that is happening in heaven now. Another variation combines the two and says that the Millennium refers to all righteousness within the kingdom of God both on earth and in heaven. We will look at this subject in more depth in a later chapter.

What Is the Great Tribulation?

The Great Tribulation is a period of intense, unprecedented suffering.

The Great Tribulation is a term Jesus used in answer to His disciples' questions about the sign of His coming and the end of the age (Matthew 24:3–22). We read in Mark 13:19, "For in those

days there will be tribulation, such as has not been from the beginning of creation which God created until this time, nor ever
shall be." In Luke 21:23, we read, "But woe to those who are
pregnant and to those who are nursing babies in those days! For
there will be great distress in the land and wrath upon this people."

Many Bible scholars who lean toward a symbolic interpretation believe that this prediction was fulfilled in AD 70 when the
Roman Emperor Titus sacked Jerusalem. Others, many of whom
lean toward a literal interpretation, combine this with other Bible
prophecies, such as Daniel 9:24–27, and understand it to be a literal period of time in the future lasting seven years, in which
there will be worldwide, unprecedented suffering.

**Bible scholars hold
either to symbolic
or to literal views
about the
Millennium and the
Great Tribulation.**

Credible arguments exist for both the symbolic and the literal interpretation of the Millennium and the Great Tribulation. We will
look more closely in later chapters at both arguments. Again, for now, our goal is simply to
become familiar with the terms.

Even those who interpret the Great Tribu-
lation literally do not completely agree about when it will occur,
or when the Rapture will occur in relationship to the Tribulation.
Some believe that the Rapture will occur immediately before the
seven-year Great Tribulation. Others believe the Rapture will
come exactly in the middle of the Great Tribulation. And still
others believe that the Rapture will come at the end of the Great
Tribulation. These rapture theories are known as pretribulation,
midtribulation, and posttribulation, respectively.

Who Is the Antichrist?

*The Antichrist embodies evil and is the key agent of Satan's resistance to the
plan of God in the last days.*

Although the actual term "Antichrist" occurs only in the
books written by the apostle John, the concept of an arch-oppo-
nent of God and Jesus the Messiah is found in several places in
the Bible. As in much prophetic literature, however, it is difficult
to establish without question what or who the Antichrist is, because in some instances the Bible seems to speak of the Antichrist as a spirit or an attitude rather than as a person. For ex-

ample, in 1 John 4:3, we read, "every spirit that does not confess that Jesus Christ has come in the flesh is not of God. And this is the spirit of the Antichrist, which you have heard was coming, and is now already in the world."

However, at other times it refers to an individual. For example, in 2 Thessalonians 2:3–4, we read:

> Let no one deceive you by any means; for that Day will not come unless the falling away comes first, and the man of sin is revealed, the son of perdition, who opposes and exalts himself above all that is called God or that is worshipped, so that he sits as God in the temple of God, showing himself that he is God.

Apparently, this is an individual, someone who makes an exclusive claim to deity. And in 2 Thessalonians 2:8–10, we read that this individual deceives many people by doing stupendous miracles, and this gets undiscerning people to believe in him:

> And then the lawless one will be revealed, whom the Lord will consume with the breath of His mouth and destroy with the brightness of His coming. The coming of the lawless one is according to the working of Satan, with all power, signs, and lying wonders, and with all unrighteous deception among those who perish, because they did not receive the love of the truth, that they might be saved.

The confusion as to whether this Antichrist is a single individual or a spirit of lawlessness pervading the end times is furthered when the apostle John says that many antichrists have already come into the world. "Little children, it is the last hour; and as you have heard that the Antichrist is coming, even now many antichrists have come, by which we know that is the last hour" (1 John 2:18). This passage seems to refer to both a spirit of Antichrist and a single Antichrist who is the archenemy of God.

This ambivalence about the nature of the Antichrist (an individual or a spirit of lawlessness) is not new to our time. It has been a topic for many reformers and church fathers throughout church history.

Both symbolic and literal views of Antichrist are held by Christians.

The symbolic view that the Antichrist is an ageless personification of evil and not identifiable with any one individual, institution, or nation, has been popular among those who emphasize the constant warfare between Satan's forces and God's.

People who interpret Scripture literally say that the symbolic view fails to stress sufficiently the passages that identify the Antichrist as an individual. They believe that the Antichrist will be a key leader in the rebellion of the world against God in the end, and they believe that this individual will usher in the Great Tribulation at history's close.

In prophetic literature, the Antichrist seems to be identified as one of two beasts mentioned in Revelation, and he has an unholy cohort, the False Prophet. Both these shadowy figures are difficult to define. Some believe they are part of the imagery in the conflict between good and evil, portraying the constancy of the warfare between Satan's forces and Christ's (*Evangelical Theological Dictionary*, 56). Other Christians believe that these shadowy figures are specific persons or beings who will appear on earth at a specific time and place. According to the latter view, the Antichrist/Beast and the False Prophet are Satan's agents, who assist him in his attempt to rule the world during the Great Tribulation.

The Beast is mentioned in the Bible (Revelation 13:1–18; 17:10–13) and is apparently a political king who dominates many political rulers and leads their combined forces to do the will of Satan.

The False Prophet (Revelation 16:13; 19:20; 20:10) is another evil being under both Antichrist's authority and the authority of the dragon, Satan (Revelation 13:2, 4). The False Prophet performs miracles to advance the cause of the Antichrist. After directing the Antichrist's political and religious enterprises, the False Prophet meets a dreadful fate along with the Antichrist/Beast when Christ returns (Revelation 19:20).

What Is the Judgment Seat of Christ?

The judgment seat of Christ is the place where all Christians will receive their reward for the quality of their lives on earth.

There are two fundamental perspectives on divine judgment. Those who believe in a literal Rapture and a literal Great Tribulation also believe that there will be two judgments: one of Christians at the "judgment seat of Christ" and one of non-Christians at the "Great White Throne judgment." The judgment seat of Christ takes place immediately after the Rapture and is about rewards in heaven, not one's eternal destiny. Only those who are true Christians will be raptured, so the issue of personal salvation is not at stake. What is at stake is the character, nature, and degrees of rewards given to Christians because of the character of their life work.

The other perspective is outlined below, and both will be discussed in greater detail in later chapters.

What Is the Great White Throne Judgment?

The Great White Throne judgment is the place where all who have rejected God will receive the punishment for their unbelief and their life on earth.

The Great White Throne judgment takes place after the Great Tribulation and after the one-thousand-year Millennium. At the end of this time, all unrighteous people will be resurrected and will be formally condemned to an eternity without God because they rejected Him during their lives.

Those who interpret these passages symbolically see only one judgment at the end of time when Christ comes back to earth and all people—Christians and non-Christians—are raised and stand before the throne of God. Christians are given rewards for their good deeds and enter heaven. Non-Christians are assigned to punishment for their evil deeds and are placed in hell.

What Are Heaven and Hell?

Heaven and hell are the ultimate destinations of all people, depending on whether or not they truly believe in God.

Again, we will deal with these subjects in greater detail in subsequent chapters, but here we want to identify the terms and see how they relate to the other prophetic events.

One of the key questions that we will be investigating later is how literally the images of heaven and hell are to be taken by Christians. Throughout church history, the two images have been taken very literally. The dominant view is of heaven as a place of gold streets, pearl gates, and fabulous mansions; and of hell as a literal lake of fire, hotter than an erupting volcano.

> **Symbolic interpretations of heaven and hell have found credence among scholars and ordinary Christians.**

In recent years, a more symbolic interpretation of these two biblical images has found credence among both serious scholars

and earnest Christians. This is causing a major reevaluation of
the nature of the eternal destiny of mankind, and the issue must
be investigated by the Christian who wants to be true to our
Lord's teachings.

Conclusion

A fundamental issue in interpreting prophecy is how literally to take the biblical passages. There are two major interpretations—the symbolic and the literal—even among earnest, sincere
Christians. One's perspective of future events will be quite different depending on which position is held.

In the remaining chapters of this book, we will discuss
events that are only valid if a person interprets biblical prophecy
literally. However, in order for readers to have a complete picture of both interpretations, the views of both camps must be
presented.

If one interprets certain prophetic passages symbolically, a
future time-line would look like this:

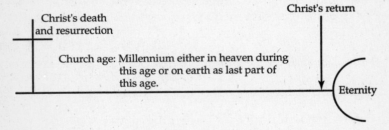

If one interprets those same prophetic passages literally, a future time-line would look like this:

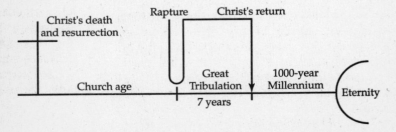

There are variations on both of these time-lines, which we will look at in subsequent chapters. The two time-lines above are held by the majority and must be understood even if variant positions are held.

Speed Bump!

Slow down to be sure you've gotten the main points of this chapter.

Question
Answer

Q1. What is the Second Coming?

A1. The Second Coming is the *return* of Christ to the earth at an unknown time in the future.

Q2. What is the Rapture?

A2. The Rapture is the sudden *departure* of all Christians to meet Christ in the air.

Q3. What is the Millennium?

A3. The Millennium refers to a period of time in when Christ reigns in *righteousness*.

Q4. What is the Great Tribulation?

A4. The Great Tribulation is a period of intense, unprecedented *suffering*.

Q5. Who is the Antichrist?

A5. The Antichrist embodies evil and is the key *agent* of Satan's resistance to the plan of God in the last days.

Q6. What is the judgment seat of Christ?

A6. The judgment seat of Christ is the place where all *Christians* will receive their reward for the quality of their lives on earth.

Q7. What is the Great White Throne judgment?

A7. The Great White Throne judgment is the place where all who have *rejected* God will receive the punishment for their unbelief and their life on earth.

Q8. What are heaven and hell?

A8. Heaven and hell are the ultimate *destinations* of all people, depending on whether or not they truly believe in God.

Fill in the Blank

Question **Q1.** What is the Second Coming of Christ?

Answer **A1.** The Second Coming is the _____ of Christ to the earth at an unknown time in the future.

Q2. What is the Rapture?

A2. The Rapture is the sudden _____ of all Christians to meet Christ in the air.

Q3. What is the Millennium?

A3. The Millennium refers to a period of time when Christ reigns in _____.

Q4. What is the Great Tribulation?

A4. The Great Tribulation is a period of intense, unprecedented _____.

Q5. Who is the Antichrist?

A5. The Antichrist embodies evil and is the key _____ of Satan's resistance to the plan of God in the last days.

Q6. What is the judgment seat of Christ?

A6. The judgment seat of Christ is the place where all _____ will receive their reward for the quality of their life on earth.

Q7. What is the Great White Throne judgment?

A7. The Great White Throne judgment is the place where all who have _____ God will receive the punishment for their unbelief and their life on earth.

Q8. What are heaven and hell?

A8. Heaven and hell are the ultimate _____ of all people, depending on whether or not they truly believe in God.

For Further Thought and Discussion

1. How many of these terms were new to you? How many were familiar? Did you have any misconceptions about these events before studying them?

2. If this is mostly new to you, what is the most significant thing you have learned by this initial look at the key terms of Bible prophecy?

3. If you were familiar with these terms, what new understanding have you gained, for instance, from looking at the different prophetic perspectives?

What If I Don't Believe?

If I don't believe it is important to gain a clear understanding of these terms regarding future things, I will remain ignorant about an entire field of study in the Scripture. I may possibly put myself at odds with my brothers and sisters in Christ. Prophecy is a difficult subject, but one which I must master if I am to have a mature understanding of Scripture.

For Further Study

1. Scripture

A number of Scripture passages are central to understanding the key terms of prophecy. They include:

- Second Coming—Acts 1:11

- Rapture—1 Thessalonians 4:13–18

- Millennium—Revelation 20:1–10

- Great Tribulation—Matthew 24:1–22

- Antichrist—1 John 2:18

- Judgment seat of Christ—2 Corinthians 5:9–10

- Great White Throne judgment—Revelation 20:11–15

- Heaven—Revelation 4:1–11

- Hell—Matthew 10:28

2. Books

There are other books which are helpful in studying these subjects. They include:

Know What You Believe, Paul Little (Literal perspective of prophecy)
A Survey of Bible Doctrine, Charles Ryrie (Literal perspective of prophecy)
Essential Truths of the Christian Faith, R. C. Sproul (Less literal perspective of prophecy)
Concise Theology, J. I. Packer (Less literal perspective of prophecy)

Many Christians long for the Rapture, not because of their intense love for the Lord, but because it gives them an escape from the distress of our age.
■ **Erwin Lutzer**

5

What Are the Major Views on the Rapture?

After graduating from high school, I attended a large state university for one year. While there, my behavior was not exemplary, and I had an undistinguished academic record. I had been a pretty moral kid in high school, but I buckled at the knees under the enticing peer pressure in college. I believed in God but had not made a firm commitment to follow Him. G.K. Chesterton, a deceased English wit, once said that when someone stops believing in God, he doesn't believe in nothing, he starts believing in everything. That was me. I started believing in everything. I started thinking that I could believe in God and live like the devil, and God would somehow understand. He would look the other way, especially if I didn't really want to live like the devil, which I didn't in my good moments. I found, however, that, as someone has said, "I could resist everything but temptation." And when I fell, this troubled me greatly.

In this chapter we learn that . . .

1. The Great Tribulation is a period of intense suffering and divine judgment in the last days.
2. Pretribulationists believe the Rapture will occur before the Great Tribulation.
3. Midtribulationists believe the Rapture will occur in the middle of the Great Tribulation.
4. Posttribulationists believe that the Rapture will occur after the Great Tribulation.

My moral struggles led to overwhelming guilt, and this led to a search for meaning in life, for an investigation of God and Jesus, which led to my salvation. After becoming a Christian, I decided intuitively that I would never survive my "new bath" if I stayed in the moral mud. I transferred to a small Christian liberal arts college, where I felt that my new faith would be nurtured and expanded. The school was steeped in prophetic awareness, and there I was taught that the Rapture could occur at any moment and that we needed always to be ready. I was so impressed by this teaching that one night I had an experience that I remember vividly. I call it my Great Shout. I awoke myself from a deep sleep by shouting. I had never done it before and have never done it since. For some reason, I concluded that, even though I was the one who shouted, this was the shout before the Rapture, mentioned in 1 Thessalonians 4:16, and that since I was not immediately taken to heaven, I must have missed the Rapture. It was an unnerving experience that I didn't get over until school started the next day and I saw that everyone else was still there.

I have had a keen interest in the Rapture ever since.

Why I need to know this

I need to understand the various positions on the Great Tribulation and the Rapture so that the biblical passages about these events will not be a complete mystery to me. I need to develop a conviction about these events and live consistently with that conviction.

There are many unanswered questions about the Rapture, which creates many different perspectives on it. We touched on them briefly in the previous chapter. Here we will look more closely at a related area, the Great Tribulation, and then we will look more closely at the three major views about the Rapture. For those readers for whom this material is familiar, it may seem as though we are laboring the issues. However, for the readers for whom this is new, the variables are so complex that an adequate review and foundational information is essential.

To understand the Rapture, we must also understand the Great Tribulation, since the two are linked together in prophecy. We will begin our study of the Rapture, then, by looking first at the Great Tribulation.

What Is the Great Tribulation?

The Great Tribulation is a period of intense suffering and divine judgment in the last days.

Some Christians believe that the references in the Bible to a Great Tribulation were fulfilled historically in AD 70 with the destruction of Jerusalem by Rome. Others believe it is symbolic of the present suffering in the world. Still others believe the Great Tribulation is a future event which will be the darkest time in human history. According to this futuristic position, more than one half of the world's population will be killed. The earth will be decimated by political and environmental cataclysms, some natural and some manmade. Earthquakes, famine, disease, and war will predominate, leaving both humanity and the globe on the verge of annihilation.

Understood literally, the Great Tribulation will be the darkest time in human history.

Those who hold to this view expect several key passages to be fulfilled literally in the future. For example, when Jesus said, "For then there will be great tribulation, such as has not been since the beginning of the world until this time, no, nor ever shall be. And unless those days were shortened, no flesh would be saved; but for the elect's sake those days will be shortened" (Matthew 24:21–22).

Of this time the prophet Daniel said, "And there shall be a time of trouble, such as never was since there was a nation, even to that time" (Daniel 12:1). The prophet Joel wrote, "For the day of the Lord is coming, for it is at hand: a day of darkness and gloominess, a day of clouds and thick darkness, like the morning clouds spread over the mountains. A people come, great and strong, the like of whom has never been; nor will there ever be any such after them, even for many successive generations" (Joel 2:1–2).

The Timetable of the Great Tribulation

The Great Tribulation is divided into two parts: the first three and one-half years, which is a time of relative calm, and the last three and one-half years, which is a time of dreadful calamity. The Great Tribulation begins with the signing of a covenant between the Antichrist and the Jews for a period of seven years (Daniel 9:27). This treaty will guarantee protection to

Israel so that they may rebuild their temple and reestablish their system of ritual sacrifice (Revelation 11:1–2). The Antichrist will try to settle the long-standing Arab-Israeli conflict and will side with Israel in their claim to the land of Palestine.

During the first three years, which unfold uneventfully, with relative peace and harmony, the Lord commissions two witnesses (Revelation 11:3) to testify of God and perform astonishing miracles.

In the middle of the seven years, the Antichrist breaks his treaty with Israel and persecutes Jews in an unprecedented manner (Daniel 9:27). He sets up an image of himself for people to worship (Matthew 24:15; 2 Thessalonians 2:4; Revelation 13:14). He kills the two witnesses and leaves their dead bodies in the streets for people to see (Revelation 11:8–10). Whoever does not worship the Antichrist/Beast is killed by one of his lieutenants, the second Beast of Revelation 13. An effort is launched to force everyone to receive the mark of the Beast, which is a sign of one's acceptance of him, and no one can buy or sell without this mark (Revelation 13:11–12, 15–17).

The Antichrist forms a coalition with the military powers of the Western world, and possibly Russia and/or other nations, to go to war against a 200-million-soldier army from the East (possibly China). The armies will meet on the plains of Megiddo in northern Israel.

Christ returns at that time (Revelation 1:7) with the armies of heaven. Heaven will open and Christ, the rider on the white horse, whose name is the "King of Kings and Lord of Lords," will lead the armies of heaven against the armies of the world's nations. The armies of the nations will be defeated, and the Antichrist and his False Prophet will be cast alive into the lake of fire (Revelation 19:11–20).

The Great Tribulation: Literal View

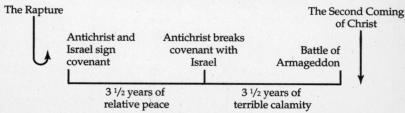

In the Book of Revelation, many events during the Great Tribulation are described as a series of three judgments of God: the judgment of the seven seals, the judgment of the seven trumpets, and the judgment of the seven bowls.

The Judgment of the Seven Seals

The first seal: a white horse represents the Antichrist who comes to conquer the Jews (Revelation 6:1–2).

The second seal: a red horse represents bloodshed and takes away peace from the earth (Revelation 6:3–4).

The third seal: a black horse represents bleak and devastating famine that comes upon the earth (Revelation 6:5–6).

The fourth seal: a pale horse represents death and one-fourth of the world's population will be killed (Revelation 6:7–8).

The fifth seal: represents the martyrdom of people who are slain for the Word of God and the testimony they held (Revelation 6:9–11).

The sixth seal: represents cataclysmic physical upheavals, such as a titanic earthquake, the sun becoming black, the moon becoming like blood, and people hiding to escape the calamities (Revelation 6:12–17).

The seventh seal: appears to be a period of ominous silence preceding dramatic thunder, lightning, and an earthquake (Revelation 8:1–5).

The Judgment of the Seven Trumpets

After the seal judgments are the seven trumpet judgments, each one indicating the beginning of a new judgment.

The first trumpet: hail and fire mingled with blood, a third of the trees will be burned up, and all green grass will be burned (Revelation 8:7).

The second trumpet: a great mountain burning with fire is dropped into the sea and one-third of the sea becomes blood, one-third of the animals in the sea die, and one-third of all ships are destroyed (Revelation 8:8–9).

The third trumpet: a burning star falls on a third of the rivers and springs, turning a third of the waters bitter, and many die from the poison (Revelation 8:10–11).

The fourth trumpet: a third of the sun is struck, as is a third of the moon and a third of the stars, so that a third of the stars became dark and a third of the day and night did not shine (Revelation 8:12–13).

The fifth trumpet: hideous creatures arise from a bottomless pit and torment people, who will desire to die, but who will not be able to (Revelation 9:1–12).

The sixth trumpet: a large army of 200 million horsemen will kill one-third of the population. This is the second time a large number of people are killed. The first was under the fourth seal, when one-fourth of the people will be killed (Revelation 6:8), and now one-third of those remaining will be killed (Revelation 19:13–21).

The seventh trumpet: signals the ending events of this terrible time and the worship of God in heaven (Revelation 11:15–19).

The Judgment of the Seven Bowls

This is the third series of judgments, also called the seven last plagues, in which the "wrath of God is completed" (Revelation 15:1).

The first bowl: people who have taken the mark of the Beast and who have worshiped his image receive a "foul and loathsome sore" (Revelation 16:2).

The second bowl: the sea becomes like the blood of a dead person and every living creature in the sea dies (Revelation 16:3).

The third bowl: the rivers and the springs turn to blood (Revelation 16:4).

The fourth bowl: the sun scorches people with oppressive heat (Revelation 16:8–9).

The fifth bowl: darkness covers the earth and people are in great pain (Revelation 16:10–11).

The sixth bowl: the Euphrates River dries up and demonic beings influence world leaders to meet for a great and dreadful war (Revelation 16:12–16).

The seventh bowl: there are great thunderstorms, the most severe earthquake ever experienced, and huge hailstones (Revelation 16:17–21).

When these three sets of seven judgments are seen all together, it is no wonder that, if they are literal events, this period is called the Great Tribulation.

What Is the Pretribulation View on the Rapture?

Pretribulationists believe the Rapture will occur before the Great Tribulation.

Four main reasons are given for this conviction.

1. *The church is promised deliverance.* In Revelation 3:10, we read, "Because you have kept My command to persevere, I also will keep you from the hour of trial which shall come upon the whole world, to test those who dwell on the earth."

    Many people believe that this promise is only to the first-century church in Philadelphia. Pretribulationists believe, however, that while there was a fundamental message given to that historic church, the language of the promise goes beyond local persecution and includes worldwide persecution that would logically occur during the Great Tribulation.

2. *The church is not appointed to wrath.* In 1 Thessalonians 5:9 we read, "For God did not appoint us to wrath, but to obtain salvation through our Lord Jesus Christ." Pretribulationists believe that Paul is speaking about the wrath that is to come on the unsaved at the end of this age during the Great Tribulation.

3. *The church is not mentioned during the Great Tribulation.* Pretribulationists believe that the church, which is mentioned in Revelation 1–3, is in heaven in Revelation 4. And in the remaining chapters of Revelation there is no mention of the church; this is interpreted as meaning that the church is absent from earth during the Great Tribulation.

4. *The church is to be ready for the imminent return of Jesus Christ.* This means that the Rapture can occur at any moment and that Christians should be constantly watching for Jesus' return.

In the pretribulation view, the church is in heaven in Revelation 4.

Titus 2:11–13 says that "the grace of God that brings salvation has appeared to all men, teaching us that, denying ungodliness and worldly lusts, we should live soberly, righteously, and godly in the present age, looking for the blessed hope and glorious appearing of our great God and Savior Jesus Christ." Verses like these point to the Rapture as the next prophetic event, not to anything else we should look for before the Rapture.

When Will the Rapture Occur?
The Pretribulation View

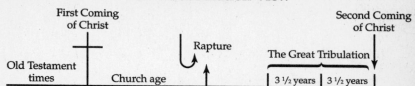

What Is the Midtribulation View on the Rapture?

Midtribulationists believe the Rapture will occur in the middle of the Great Tribulation.

Midtribulationists agree with pretribulationists that the church will not experience the wrath of God during the Great Tribulation. But they differ as to when the wrath of God begins. Midtribulationists see the Great Tribulation occurring during the first three and a half years of the seven-year period, and they see the wrath of God poured out during the last three and a half years. In this view, the church is present during the Great Tribulation, but she is raptured before God's wrath is poured out.

The Great Tribulation will be dreadful but brief. "For then there will be great tribulation, such as has not been since the beginning of the world until this time, no, nor ever shall be. And unless those days were shortened, no flesh would be saved; but for the elect's sake those days will be shortened" (Matthew 24:21–22).

As dreadful as the Great Tribulation will be, midtribulationists say that it should not be confused with the time of God's wrath. The Great Tribulation is severe, but it is brief enough that the elect will not perish. Christians are spared the wrath of God.

In the midtribulation view, opinions vary as to when God's wrath begins.

But disagreement exists among midtribulationists as to terminology and to the timing of the Rapture. Some place the Rapture immediately before the seventh trumpet (Revelation 11:15). This means that the time of wrath for the ungodly and the time of rewards for the unrighteous dead occur simultaneously.

Other midtribulationists insist that the Great Tribulation

does not begin until the last three and a half years. Whatever words are employed, the agreed upon concept is the same. The church is present during the first half of the seven-year period undergoing persecution and troubles that are, by comparison to the last half, relatively light. The church is then raptured before the wrath of God is poured out.

When Will the Rapture Occur?
The Midtribulation View

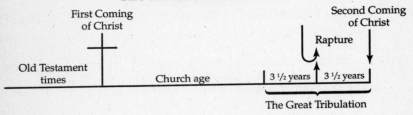

What Is the Posttribulation Rapture?

Posttribulationists believe that the Rapture will occur after the Great Tribulation.

Generally, posttribulationists believe that Christians will go through the entire Great Tribulation and that Christ will return at the end of it. Some posttribulationists see a distinction between the Rapture and the Second Coming and some do not. When a distinction is seen, the time between the two is very short. Essentially, the event predicted in 1 Thessalonians 4, where Christians are caught up to meet the Lord in the air, happens in "the twinkling of an eye." And immediately after that they return to earth with Christ to fulfill the prediction of His second coming. Others see the passage in 1 Thessalonians as describing the first stage of His second coming, and they do not believe it describes the Rapture. In either event, Christ's return ends the Great Tribulation and begins the Millennium.

To elaborate, the first major distinction of posttribulation view is that the church will not be raptured prior to the middle of the Great Tribulation but will go through it and endure it by the grace and protection of God. Only then will Jesus Christ come.

The pretribulation view argues that the church will not be

exposed to God's wrath and cites key passages to validate the point. The posttribulation view agrees with this, but it sees the escape from wrath quite differently. The posttribulationist says that the Christians will be preserved from God's wrath while going through the Great Tribulation. The pretribulationist says that Christians will escape God's wrath by being raptured before it happens.

The Israelites in Egypt are often cited as the example of this. The plagues on Egypt were applied selectively. They came upon the Egyptians and not the Israelites. So it will be with God's wrath during the Great Tribulation. The plagues and calamities that fall upon the earth will be applied to non-Christians, and Christians will be preserved in the midst of the trouble rather than being taken out it.

Noah is another example that is frequently cited. He and his family were not taken out of the world. They were left to endure the great flood, but God saved them from calamity even while it was falling on everyone else. This is why posttribulationists believe that Christians will go through the Great Tribulation without experiencing the wrath of God.

At the end of the Great Tribulation, Christ returns in two stages. He comes *for* the church and then He returns *with* the church. In a posttribulationist view, all passages that refer to a coming of the Lord are about those nearly simultaneous events. This will conclude the Great Tribulation and establish the physical kingdom of God on earth and usher in the millennial reign.

Posttribulationists are often less literal in their approach to biblical prophecy than pretribulationists. For example, many posttribulationists are not sure that the Great Tribulation will be precisely seven calendar years. They are also unsure as to the length of the Millennium; it may not be exactly a thousand years. They do agree, however, that the Great Tribulation lasts for an extended period which Christians will go through, and that the Lord will personally rule on earth for an extended period of time.

In the posttribulation view, Christians will go through the Great Tribulation.

In this view, therefore, Christ could not come "any day," because the Great Tribulation and the Millennium would have to come first.

One of the primary reasons that posttribulationists do not believe the church will escape the Great Tribulation is that God's people have not been exempt from tribulation in all other periods of history. Jesus said in John 16:33, "These things I have spoken to you, that in Me you may have peace. In the world you will have tribulation; but be of good cheer, I have overcome the world."

In Acts 14:22, Paul preached that we must enter the kingdom of God through many tribulations. He even said we "glory in our tribulations" (Romans 5:3). In Revelation 1:9, the apostle John identifies himself as a brother and a companion in tribulation. And in 1 Thessalonians 3:3, Paul writes that we should not be shaken by our afflictions because we were appointed to that destiny.

In Hebrews 11, we are told that many saints of old were tortured, mocked, whipped, chained, and imprisoned; others were stoned, sawn in two, tempted, killed by the sword, wandered destitute, afflicted, and tormented. In Hebrews 12:1, we read, "Therefore we also, since we are surrounded by so great a cloud of witnesses [that is, these saints who have gone on before us], let us lay aside every weight, and the sin which so easily ensnares us, and let us run with endurance the race that is set before us."

When Will the Rapture Occur?
The Posttribulation View

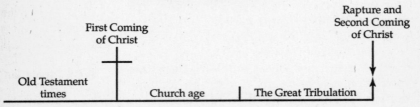

Conclusion

There are two basic views about the Great Tribulation: 1) it was fulfilled historically around AD 70 with the destruction of Jerusalem; 2) it will occur in the future.

There are two basic views on the Rapture: 1) it is the same thing as, or happens at the same time as, the Second Coming; 2) it is different from the Second Coming and separated from it by a debatable amount of time. Of those who hold to the latter view, some believe it will occur before the Great Tribulation; some believe it will occur in the middle of the Great Tribulation; some believe it will occur at the end of the Great Tribulation.

Speed Bump!

Slow down to be sure you've gotten the main points of this chapter.

Question
Answer

Q1. What is the Great Tribulation?

A1. The Great Tribulation is a period of intense suffering and divine *judgment* in the last days.

Q2. What is the pretribulation view on the Rapture?

A2. Pretribulationists believe the Rapture will occur *before* the Great Tribulation.

Q3. What is the midtribulation view on the Rapture?

A3. Midtribulationists believe the Rapture will occur in the *middle* of the Great Tribulation.

Q4. What is the posttribulation view on the Rapture?

A4. Posttribulationists believe that the Rapture will occur *after* the Great Tribulation.

Fill in the Blank

Question
Answer

Q1. What is the Great Tribulation?

A1. The Great Tribulation is a period of intense suffering and divine _____ in the last days.

Q2. What is the pretribulation view on the Rapture?

A2. Pretribulationists believe the Rapture will occur _____ the Great Tribulation.

Q3. What is the midtribulation view on the Rapture?

A3. Midtribulationists believe the Rapture will occur in the _____ of the Great Tribulation.

Q4. What is the posttribulation view on the Rapture?

A4. Posttribulationists believe that the Rapture will occur _____
the Great Tribulation.

For Further Thought and Discussion

1. What difference do you think it makes whether a person believes the
Rapture is different from the Second Coming or the same thing as the
Second Coming? Would that person live any differently holding to one
view or the other? Would the two views influence the person in other
ways?

2. What difference do you think it makes whether a person believes the
Rapture comes before, in the middle of, or after the Great Tribulation?
Would the person live any differently holding to one or the other view?
Would the three views influence the person other ways?

What If I Don't Believe?

If I don't have an understanding of the Rapture or Great Tribulation, I
may get lost when trying to understand some passages of Scripture. I may
also have misunderstandings with other Christians who have other assumptions than mine. However, regardless of our understanding and convictions,
the commands of Scripture remain the same. I am to love God with all my
heart, soul, and mind, and my neighbor as myself. I am to live as though He
were coming today, but plan as though He were not coming in my lifetime. I
need to strive to "keep the unity of the spirit in the bond of peace" (Ephesians
4:3).

For Further Study

1. Scripture
*There are two key passages that are central to understanding this subject. They
are:*

- 1 Thessalonians 4:13–18

- Matthew 24:1–26

2. Books

There are other books which are helpful in studying this subject further. They include:

Doomsday Delusions, C. Marvin Pate and Calvin B. Haines, Jr.
Contemporary Options in Eschatology, Millard Erickson
The Pre-Wrath Rapture, Marvin Rosenthal

*The only way to wait for the Second Coming is to
watch that you do what you should do, so that when
he comes it is a matter of indifference.*
■ **Oswald Chambers (1874–1917)**

What Are the Three Major Views on the Millennium?

William Shakespeare wrote that life is "a tale told by an idiot, full of sound and fury, signifying nothing" (*Macbeth*, Act V, v). Many people throughout history have, in less eloquent words, said the same thing. G.N. Clark, past president of Cambridge University, is reported to have said at his inauguration, "There is no secret and no plan in history to be discovered. I do not believe that any future consummation could make any sense of all the irrationalities of preceding ages. If it could not explain them, still less could it justify them." In the introduction to his *A History of Europe*, H.A.L. Fisher wrote, "One intellectual excitement has been denied me. Men wiser and more learned than I am have discovered in history a plot, a rhythm, a pattern. But these harmonies are concealed from me. I can see only one emergency following another, as wave follows upon wave . . ."

When God is taken out of history, little history has any meaning,

When God is removed from history, little history has any meaning.

and there is even less to suggest that history is moving toward a predetermined and good end. Therefore, in the last two hundred years, as thinkers have done away with God, they have had a difficult time maintaining meaning or optimism about life. George Orwell, a leading thinker dedicated to doing away with God, wrote in 1944, "For two hundred years we had sawed and sawed and sawed at the branch we were sitting on. And in the end, much more suddenly than anyone had foreseen, our efforts were rewarded, and down we came. But unfortunately there had been a little mistake: The thing at the bottom was not a bed of roses after all, it was a cesspool of barbed wire. . . . It appears that amputation of the soul isn't just a simple surgical job, like having your appendix out. The wound has a tendency to go septic [become infected]."

One of the symptoms of "going septic" has been a collapse of meaning, purpose, and positive destiny for humanity. Orwell wrote, "Since about 1930 the world has given no reason for optimism whatever. Nothing is in sight except a welter of lies, hatred, cruelty, and ignorance, and beyond our present troubles loom vaster ones which are only now entering into the . . . consciousness. It is quite possible that man's major problems will never be solved" (cited in *Christianity Today*, January 13, 1984, 25–26).

In this chapter we learn that . . .

1. Premillennialism is the belief that the Second Coming of Christ will inaugurate a literal period of 1,000 years during which Christ will rule over the world as its political leader.
2. Postmillennialism is the belief that the Gospel will spread throughout the earth creating a better and better world, after which Jesus returns to bring this age to a close and usher in eternity.
3. Amillennialism is the belief that the thousand-year reign of Christ is purely symbolic of the ultimate triumph of God's righteousness and goodness in the world.

How bleak is the future for those who do not believe in God; they have no true hope! Without God, there is no hope. Yet the Bible tells us of a creation that is moving toward a predetermined end, which will be good for those who believe in God and accept His salvation. In the end, God's children will be delivered from an earth that will self-destruct because of the sinfulness of humanity.

Against the bleakness of the above humanist perspective, the Christian perspective is that of a brilliant sun rising above low, dark clouds of the end. Christianity does not deny bleakness and misfortune, but it also teaches that one day bleakness and misfortune will end and a new, glorious day will arise. In that day God will right all that has gone wrong because of sin. Paradise will be restored. Those who truly believe in God will enter it. Those who do not will not.

As history moves toward this triumph of good over evil, Christians understand the culmination in different ways. But they are all agreed on the premise. *Good* will ultimately triumph.

The beginning of this triumph, in the understanding of many Christians, is the Millennium, the thousand-year reign of Jesus Christ on the earth mentioned in Revelation 20:1–6. Most Christians hold to one of three perspectives on the Millennium.

Why I need to know this

I need to know the various millennial views so that I can properly understand these passages of Scripture and gain confidence and comfort from the position I hold. I also need to understand others who hold to a different millennial view.

What Is Premillennialism?

Premillennialism is the belief that the Second Coming of Christ will inaugurate a literal period of 1,000 years during which Christ will rule over the world as its political leader.

Premillenialism is founded on the conviction that the Bible should be interpreted *literally* whenever doing so does not lead to an absurd conclusion. When Jesus says, "I am the door" (John 10:9), or, "I am the bread of life" (John 6:35), the premillennialist does not envision a six-foot-tall oak tree or loaf of bread! Those references are symbolic (see John 10:6). However, unless it is clear that a passage is to be understood symbolically, it is typically interpreted literally by the premillennialist.

The Abrahamic Covenant

This conviction about a literal interpretation of Scripture has its greatest bearing on Bible prophecy when it comes to the Abrahamic covenant. Premillennialists interpret this literally, and that affects all other prophecy. In Genesis 12:1–3, God made a covenant with Abraham:

> Now the Lord had said to Abram: "Get out of your country, from your kindred and from your father's house, to a land that I will show you. I will make you a great nation; I will bless you and make your name great; and you shall be a blessing. I will bless those who bless you, and I will curse him who curses you; and in you all the families of the earth shall be blessed."

Other passages in Genesis reiterate and expand this initial covenant (Genesis 13:14–17; 15:1–7; 17:1–18). This covenant to Abraham promises dramatic blessing. God told Abraham that He would . . .

(1) give him land,
(2) many descendants, and

(3) that He would not only bless Abraham richly, but that He would bless the whole world through Abraham.

Two of these promises were literally fulfilled: Abraham had many descendants, numbered in the millions, and he was richly blessed with wealth, land, servants, cattle, silver, and gold (Genesis 13:14–15; 17; 15:7; 24:34, 35). Also, Abraham was richly blessed by a close relationship with God; he was called a friend of God (Genesis 18:17; James 2:23). And God's promise to bless the entire world through Abraham was fulfilled in Jesus, who was from the lineage of Abraham and who became a blessing to the entire world. So all these promises were fulfilled literally.

Literal Fulfillment of the Abrahamic Covenant

The promise of *all* the land, however, has not yet been fulfilled literally. God promised to give Abraham's descendants land whose boundaries were clearly specified, and that land would be an everlasting possession for them. "On the same day the Lord made a covenant with Abram, saying: 'To your descendants I have given this land, from the river of Egypt to the great river, the River Euphrates . . .' " (Genesis 15:18). "Also I give to you and your descendants after you the land in which you are a stranger, all the land of Canaan, as an everlasting possession; and I will be their God" (Genesis 17:8).

The boundaries of this are "from the river of Egypt to the great river, the River Euphrates" (Genesis 15:18). The eastern boundary is the Euphrates River, but the western boundary is not clear. Some believe that the river of Egypt refers to the Nile; others believe that it refers to the Wadi-El-Arish, not far from Gaza. In either case, Israel has never occupied that much land.

This is deeply significant to the premillennialist, because if the other promises to Abraham were fulfilled literally, then it seems consistent to believe that this promise will be fulfilled literally. If so, since it has never been fulfilled in the past, it is still to be fulfilled. This dovetails quite conveniently with the prediction of a thousand-year reign of Christ on earth in which (it is assumed) Israel will occupy the full measure of that land during the period when Jesus Christ rules the world from the glorified city of Jerusalem.

In the premillennialist view, Israel has yet to occupy *all* land promised by God.

In a brief aside, it should be noted that two passages of

Scripture are often understood to mean that the "land promises" to Abraham and his descendants have already been fully fulfilled literally. They are Joshua 21:43–45 and 1 Kings 4:21. In the first passage, the Israelites had just taken basic control over the land of Canaan:

> So the Lord gave to Israel all the land of which He had sworn to give to their fathers, and they took possession of it and dwelt in it. The Lord gave them rest all around, according to all that He had sworn to their fathers. . . . Not a word failed of any good thing which the Lord had spoken to the house of Israel. All came to pass.

According to premillennialists, this passage does not record the full fulfillment of the "land promises." In the *Bible Knowledge Commentary: Old Testament,* written by the Dallas Theological Seminary faculty, we read:

> This did not mean that every corner of the land was in Israel's possession, for God Himself had told Israel that they would conquer the land gradually (Deuteronomy 7:22). Some theologians have insisted that the statement in Joshua 21:43 means that the land promise of the Abrahamic Covenant was fulfilled then. But this cannot be true because later the Bible gives additional predictions about Israel possessing the land after the time of Joshua (e.g., Amos 9:14–15). Joshua 21:43, therefore, refers to the extent of the land as outlined in Numbers 34 and not to the ultimate extent as it will be in the messianic kingdom (Genesis 15:18–21). Also, though Israel possessed the land at this time it was later dispossessed, whereas the Abrahamic Covenant promised Israel that she would possess the land forever (Genesis 17:8) (364–365).

In 1 Kings 4:21, we have a similar situation, in which Solomon's domain is said to stretch from the Euphrates River as far as the border of Egypt, but all of this territory was not incorporated into Israel. Many of the defeated kingdoms retained their identity and paid taxes to Solomon. Israel's actual territory included the smaller region "from Dan to Beersheba" (1 Kings 4:25).

Unconditional Fulfillment of the Abrahamic Covenant

Another critical issue for the premillennialist is that the promises given to Abraham are seen as unconditional. In Genesis 15:9–17 we read:

> So He said to him, "Bring Me a three-year-old heifer, a three-year-old female goat, a three-year-old ram, a turtledove, and a young pigeon."

Then he brought all these to Him and cut them in two, down the middle, and placed each piece opposite the other; but he did not cut the birds in two. And when the vultures came down on the carcasses, Abram drove them away. Now when the sun was going down, a deep sleep fell upon Abram; and behold, horror and great darkness fell upon him. Then He said to Abram: "Know certainly that your descendants will be strangers in a land that is not theirs, and will serve them, and they will afflict them four hundred years. And also the nation whom they serve I will judge; afterward they shall come out with great possessions. Now as for you, you shall go to your fathers in peace; you shall be buried at a good old age. But in the fourth generation they shall return here, for the iniquity of the Amorites is not yet complete." And it came to pass, when the sun went down and it was dark, that behold, there was a smoking oven and a burning torch that passed between those pieces.

This is a dark and mystifying passage until it is seen in light of ancient customs for ratifying covenants. According to the tradition of the time, a covenant could be ratified by sacrificing animals, cutting them into two halves and laying the two halves on the ground opposite each other, so that there was a path between them. Then the two parties entering into the formal agreement would walk together between the halved animals, signifying their acceptance of the terms of the covenant.

In this instance, however, there is a significant departure from that practice. Instead of both God *and* Abraham walking the corridor between the severed pieces, God alone passed between them. The smoking oven and burning torch are symbolic of God's presence. This seems to indicate that this was a unilateral covenant. That is, the responsibility for the fulfillment of the threefold blessing to Abraham (see above) depended on God and God alone.

> In the premillennialist view, God will fulfill the Abrahamic covenant with Israel completely.

This covenant was reiterated to Abraham's son, Isaac, and to Isaac's son, Jacob (Genesis 26:2–4; 28:13–15). In neither reiteration were any conditions attached; both were based solely on the oath which God had made earlier with Abraham.

It is certainly true that throughout Israel's history peace in the land was conditional to the nation's obedience and that dispersion was a judgment brought about by the nation's disobedience (Deuteronomy 28:25; Jeremiah 25:11). This does not present a significant obstacle to the premillennialist, who sees these "conditions" as distinct from God's original intention to fully fulfill the land covenant with Israel. This dovetails quite nicely with the premillennialist's understanding of a thousand-year reign of righteousness by Christ on earth, during which time Israel will possess the entire promised land.

The Time-line of Premillennialism

To understand the chronology of premillennialism, it is helpful to begin with a chart.

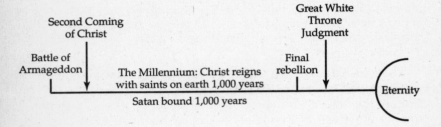

For the premillennialist, five major events dominant the Millennium.

1. *The Battle of Armageddon.* The battle of Armageddon is the last event of the Great Tribulation and the first event of the Millennium. It is a battle in which the Antichrist and all of his allied nations and their armies gather together in northern Israel for a war against God. Revelation 16:12–16 states that through the influence of demons, the kings of the earth and of the whole world gather together for a battle on the great day of God Almighty. "And they gathered them together to the place called in Hebrew, Armageddon" (verse 16).

It is uncertain what the Antichrist and his allied armies intend to do when they gather at Armageddon. Some people believe that they head to that area to wage a war with a two-hundred-million-man army, invading Israel from the east. Then, as the earthly armies prepare to do battle, Christ comes down with His army of heaven and destroys the earthly armies (Revelation 19:11–21).

The devastation from this battle is so great that much of the earth's population is killed and much of the plant life on earth is destroyed. Air and water are severely polluted.

2. *The Second Coming of Christ.* Chronologically the battle of Armageddon and the second coming of Christ occur essentially simultaneously. It is as the kings of the earth gather together in the Valley of Megiddo that Christ comes from heaven with His armies and destroys the armies of earth.

   Having returned to earth, Christ is now in a position to establish His kingdom on the earth, headquartered in Jerusalem where He will reign over the earth for the next thousand years.

3. *The thousand-year binding of Satan.* In order to facilitate His reign of righteousness on earth, Christ has an angel from heaven bind Satan and cast him into a bottomless pit, shut it up, and seal it for a thousand years, so that during the thousand-year reign of Christ on earth, Satan will not be able to deceive the nations. In Revelation 20:1–3, we read:

Then I saw an angel coming down from heaven, having the key to the bottomless pit and a great chain in his hand. He laid hold of the dragon, that serpent of old, who is the Devil and Satan, and bound him for a thousand years; and he cast him into the bottomless pit, and shut him up, and set a seal on him, so that he should deceive the nations no more till the thousand years were finished. But after these things he must be released for a little while."

4. *The one-thousand-year reign of Christ.* The earth is now ready for the political, social and spiritual Lordship of Christ. Satan has been removed from the earth, and all of his followers of significant influence have been destroyed. Jesus returns to earth with all of the Christians who have believed in Him, from His first coming until His second coming. All of these resurrected saints will be priests of God and of Christ and will reign with Him for a thousand years. In Revelation 20:4–6, we read:

And I saw thrones, and they sat on them, and judgment was committed to them. And I saw the souls of those who had been beheaded for their witness to Jesus and for the word of God, who had not worshipped the beast or his image, and had not received his mark on their foreheads or on their hands. And they lived and reigned with Christ for a thousand years. But the rest of the dead

did not live again until the thousand years were finished. This is the
first resurrection. Blessed and holy is he who has part in the first resurrection. Over such the second death has no power, but they shall
be priests of God and of Christ, and shall reign with Him a thousand
years.

The earth is then populated with two different kinds of
people. One kind are the resurrected saints; the other kind are
the unresurrected people with earthly bodies who are living
during the battle of Armageddon and who were not killed.
This latter group will include the one hundred and forty-four
thousand Jewish evangelists who were sealed by God and
commissioned to evangelize during the Great Tribulation. This
latter group will also include the people who come to know
Christ during the Great Tribulation.

The earth will be purged by the Great Tribulation and the
battle of Armageddon much like it was by the great flood in
Noah's day. The remaining people, both Jew and Gentile, live
peacefully and prosperously under the political leadership of
Jesus, who rules from His throne in Jerusalem.

**When Israel is fully
in the land, it will
be a time of
unprecedented
glory.**
Babies will be born, and as the years pass,
there will be individuals who do not accept
Christ as their Savior and Lord, even though
they will be forced to give outward allegiance
to Christ's authority. Because Satan is not
around to instigate any defiance and because
Jesus is ruling politically with "a rod of iron," the non-Christians are essentially indiscernible from the Christians.

As we saw, one of the central purposes during this thousand-year reign will be for Israel to inhabit *all* the land
promised to them in the Abrahamic covenant. Israel will finally extend from the river of Egypt to the Euphrates River,
and it will be a time of unprecedented glory as all the unfulfilled promises of God are completed literally for Israel.

5. *The final rebellion.* At the end of the Millennium, Satan is released from his prison in the bottomless pit and comes back to
the earth to instigate among all the unbelievers a final rebellion against the rule of Christ. This will be Satan's last-ditch effort to thwart the will of God on earth. It fails miserably:

Now when the thousand years have expired, Satan will be released
from his prison and will go out to deceive the nations which are in
the four corners of the earth, Gog and Magog, to gather them to-

gether to battle, whose number is as the sand of the sea. They went up on the breadth of the earth and surrounded the camp of the saints and the beloved city. And fire came down from God out of heaven and devoured them (Revelation 20:7–9).

Satan will then be cast into the lake of fire, to join the beast and the false prophet, and they will be tormented day and night forever and ever (Revelation 20:10). After this, the Great White Throne judgment takes place for those who are not believers.

While the Bible does not say much about the earth being renovated for the Millennium, it seems likely that renovation occurs. In the Great Tribulation, much of the earth is destroyed, and much of the air and water is severely polluted, so it seems likely that this devastation will have to be corrected in order for the millennial earth to be a place of unparalleled peace, prosperity, and harmony. This idea is supported in Isaiah 35:1–2:

The wilderness and the wasteland shall be glad for them, / and the desert shall rejoice and blossom as the rose; / it shall blossom abundantly and rejoice, / even with joy and singing. / The glory of Lebanon shall be given to it, / the excellence of Carmel and Sharon. / They shall see the glory of the Lord, / The excellency of our God.

This passage seems to indicate substantially increased productivity during the Millennium, which probably resulted from much of the earth's renovation. The curse resultant from Adam's sin, to which the earth and nature were subjected, is apparently reversed, though it will not be entirely lifted until the end of the Millennium. At that time, death will be vanquished forever and there will be a new heaven and a new earth. However, during this time, increased rainfall, food, and productivity will bring an era of great prosperity, and Christ's righteous rule will guarantee that all are properly paid for their products and services. Peace on earth will mean prosperity on earth and social justice for everyone.

Some premillennialists believe that a restoration of the Old Testament way of life will occur at this time. According to this view, God temporarily turned away from Israel to the church when Israel rejected Christ's offer of the kingdom during His first coming. When God has accomplished His purposes with the church, He will resume His plans with Israel. Therefore, in the Millennium, Israel will be restored to the land of Palestine. Jesus will sit upon the literal throne of David and will rule the world from Jerusalem. The Old Testament temple will be rebuilt and the Jewish system of worship will be restored, including the sacrificial system. During this time, virtually all Old Testament prophecies not fulfilled by the time of Christ's return will then be fulfilled.

Other premillennialists believe that since Christ was the perfect sacrifice the Old Testament sacrificial system will have passed away forever. While the temple and some form of Jewish worship might be established, this will not include the sacrificial system.

What Is Postmillennialism?

Postmillennialism is the belief that the Gospel will spread throughout the earth creating a better and better world after which Jesus returns to bring this age to a close and usher in eternity.

The postmillennialist has quite a different view toward the millennium than does the premillennialist. The postmillennialist does not see a literal seven-year Great Tribulation. Neither does he see a literal thousand-year Millennium with Christ ruling physically on earth to fulfill all of the as-yet unfulfilled Old Testament promises about Israel. Rather, as the Gospel spreads throughout the earth, and as people increasingly accept Christ as their savior, laws, social values, and cultural practices gradually become more and more Christian. In this way, a "millennium" gradually increases on earth as Christ-centered Christians exercise more and more Christ-centered influence over earthly affairs.

The Time-line of Postmillennialism

To understand the chronology of postmillennialism, it is helpful to begin with a chart.

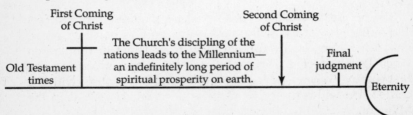

First Coming of Christ   Second Coming of Christ

Old Testament times | The Church's discipling of the nations leads to the Millennium— an indefinitely long period of spiritual prosperity on earth. | Final judgment | Eternity

The postmillennial view of Bible prophecy emphasizes four period and events:

1. Old Testament Israel. The Old Testament revealed the physical kingdom of God on earth as He worked through the nation of Israel.

2. The First Coming of Christ. The first coming of Christ, followed by His death, resurrection, and ascension, was a dramatic break with the Old Testament, in which God worked primarily through the nation Israel. The first coming and death of Christ instituted the New Testament, in which God begins to work His kingdom through the church.

3. The Church and Millennium. In the Old Testament, God's kingdom was primarily a physical kingdom, whereas in the New Testament it is primarily a spiritual kingdom on earth, though the spiritual kingdom has its undeniable influence on the physical, earthly, kingdoms. Most notably, the condition of humanity on earth improves as the gospel advances. The gospel advances with struggle and setbacks, yet it triumphs over evil. As it does, life gets better and better until peace, justice, and righteousness pervade the world.

4. The Second Coming of Christ. After an undetermined length of time, in which the principles of righteousness predominate on the earth, Jesus comes back to earth bringing history to a close.

One main distinctive of postmillennialism is the belief that the kingdom of God is primarily a present reality on earth. But it is not a physical realm or domain; it is the rule of Christ in the hearts of men and women. Wherever people believe in Christ and accept Him as their personal Savior, and live obediently, the kingdom is present. It is not something, as the premillennialists believe, that will be brought on dramatically at some time in the future.

In the postmillennial view, the kingdom of God is presently on earth.

A second major distinctive is the expectation that all the nations will turn to Christ before Jesus returns to earth. According to postmillennial beliefs, the gospel will be spread more and more effectively around the world and an increasing number of people will be converted to Christ. The result is that the condition of humanity upon the earth will get better and better. There are a number of Scripture passages used to support this postmillennial belief. In Isaiah 45:22–25, we read:

> Look to Me, and be saved, all you ends of the earth! For I am God, and there is no other. I have sworn by Myself; the word has gone out of My mouth in righteousness, and shall not return, that to Me every knee shall bow, every tongue shall take an oath. He shall say, surely in the Lord I have righteousness and strength. To Him men shall come, and all shall be ashamed who are incensed against Him. In the Lord all the descendants of Israel shall be justified, and shall glory.

While this passage speaks of God's dealing with the chosen people of Israel, it also seems to go beyond to speak of a universal acceptance of Him. Hosea 2:23 also appears to speak of God's covenant with Israel as going beyond those who are Jews.

In addition, Jesus said more than once that the Gospel would be preached to the whole world, and that this would take place before His second coming. In Matthew 24:14, we read, "And this gospel of the kingdom will be preached in all the world as a witness to all the nations, and then the end will come." Premillennialists understand this to mean that the preaching reaches all the nations but is not effective in converting all nations. Rather, it is effective in bringing men and women from every people, tribe, and tongue to salvation, but the nations in which they live will not as a whole be saved. Postmillennialists believe that Jesus' commission to take the gospel into all the world was accompanied by the statement that all power had been given unto Him (Matthew 28:18). This power would presumably result in the conversion of the people to whom the gospel was preached.

Admittedly, the spread of the gospel and the conversion of the entire world is not happening, nor is it likely to happen at a rapid pace. This does not bother postmillennialists. They have faith in what they understand to be the promise of God, and they believe that however long it takes it will ultimately be fulfilled.

Progress in the world from the time of Christ until the present time is used as supporting evidence for this postmillennial view. For example, slavery, polygamy, brutal oppression of women and children, and totalitarian governments often dominated pre-Christian cultures. Today, slavery and polygamy have been virtually eliminated, while the brutal oppression of women and children and the dominance of totalitarian governments are declining.

In addition, the technology for spreading the gospel to the entire earth is far better today than ever before, and it will likely improve in far greater ways. As the effectiveness of spreading the gospel increases, it is reasoned that the number of people who turn to Christ will increase.

Further, at present, an unprecedented number around the world are turning to Christ. The collapse of the Soviet Union resulted in one of the most dramatic opportunities for evangelism that the world has ever seen. In China, even though Christianity is presently suppressed, people are said to be turning to Christ by the millions, although the accounts are, admittedly, difficult to verify. At the same time, large churches in Korea number in the hundreds of thousands, and throughout Latin America people are turning to Christ at a rate faster than the birth rate!

> **As the gospel spreads and influences the world, it will increasingly affect political and social structures.**

Postmillennialists believe that this phenomenon is like a rock dropped into a still pond, which can and will result in waves and ripples reaching throughout these countries to eventually effect their entire political, social, and cultural structures.

What Is Amillennialism?

Amillennialism is the belief that the thousand-year reign of Christ is purely symbolic of the ultimate triumph of God's righteousness and goodness in the world.

Amillennialism, like postmillennialism, is perspective simpler than premillennialism, requiring fewer words to explain it. Amillennialists do not expect a literal thousand-year Millennium or a millennial reign of Christ on earth, either physically or spiritually. They tend to interpret prophetic Scripture symbolically, and as a consequence, they often do not expect a literal fulfillment of prophecy. They believe that many of the prophecies were either fulfilled relatively soon after they were given or else they are not to be fulfilled literally.

As a result, amillennialists tend not to study prophetic literature in an effort to pinpoint events of the end times. Their generally symbolic interpretation of prophecy is expressed in the common amillennial view that the Millennium of Revelation 20 is occurring now as Christ reigns as the risen, ascended, and exalted Lord over all of creation. Amillennialists believe that, regardless of when Jesus returns, we are to be dedicated to spiri-

tual growth, evangelism, and the advancement of kingdom principles.

The Time-line of Amillennialism

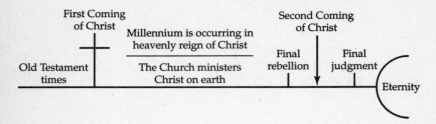

1. *Old Testament Israel.* The Old Testament is seen as God's
first covenant with Israel.

2. *The First Coming of Christ.* The first coming of Christ, along
with His death, resurrection, and ascension, brings a great break
in God's plan between the Old Testament and the New Testament.

3. *The New Testament Church.* The New Testament is God's
new covenant with the church, which supersedes His old
covenant with Israel, and many of the unfulfilled prophecies and
components of the Old Testament that were given to Israel are
fulfilled in the New Testament with the church.

4. *The Second Coming of Christ.* The second coming of Christ
ends the period of the New Testament and brings to a close history on earth as we have known it.

In some ways amillennialism is a view of the future, easier to
understand and describe than either premillennialism or postmillennialism. Basically, there will be no earthly seven-year
Great Tribulation and no thousand-year reign of Christ on earth.
Many of the prophecies that were not fulfilled literally to Israel
in the Old Testament are seen as fulfilled in the church figuratively and symbolically in the New Testament. Many prophecies
in Revelation, which to some appear to indicate a coming Great
Tribulation and a Millennium, are understood symbolically,
"picturing" rather than "predicting." Some amillennialists
would say that the conflict between good and evil is ongoing on
the earth until the second coming of Christ.

Others would say that "the kingdom of God is now present

in the world as the victorious Christ rules His church through the Word and the Spirit. The future glorious and perfect kingdom referred to in the Scriptures alludes to the new earth and life in heaven. Thus, Revelation 20, which is often seen as a very clear description of events in the Millennium, is understood by the amillennialist to be a description of the souls of dead believers reigning with Christ in heaven" (*Evangelical Dictionary of Theology,* 715).

In the amillennialist view, there is no Great Tribulation or thousand-year reign of Christ on earth.

Millard Erickson, in his book *Contemporary Options in Eschatology,* has written clearly regarding the amillennialist viewpoint of prophetic literature, particularly in the Book of Revelation:

> Another important tenet of amillennialism is its interpretation of the thousand years in Revelation 20. Verse 2 speaks of Satan being bound for a thousand years, and verse 4 of those who have been beheaded for their testimony to Jesus, reigning with Him for a thousand years. The interpretation of these two references requires first that we see the nature of the entire book and the place of this portion within it.
>
> The amillennialist generally sees Revelation as composed of several sections (usually seven), each of which recapitulates the events of the same period rather than describing the events of successive periods. Each deals with the same era—the period between Christ's first and second comings—picking up earlier themes, elaborating and developing them further. Revelation 20, then, does not speak of far-removed, future events, and the meaning of the thousand years is to be found in some past and/or present fact (19).

Further, and even more generally, the passage must be understood within the broad context of the book as a whole. One must remember that Revelation is a very symbolic and figurative book. Not even premillennialists press all of its images for literal meanings. If one would, the result would be ludicrous. When chapter 20 speaks of the binding of Satan, for example, certainly no one thinks this will be done with a literal chain of metal. Few would see the bowls, seals, and trumpets as literal. Therefore, it seems reasonable to conclude that the number "one thousand" might not be literal either.

Because amillennialists tend to interpret prophetic passages symbolically, their conclusions regarding the Millennium are quite different from those of the premillennialist or the postmillennialist.

Conclusion

What Is the Millennium? Three Views

Premillennialism

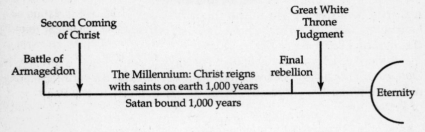

Postmillennialism

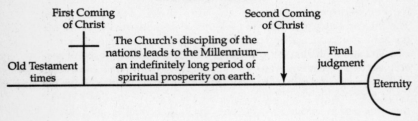

Amillennialism

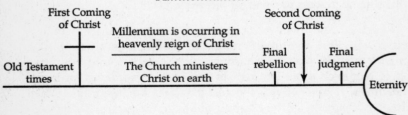

Equally bright, well-educated, spiritually mature people hold to different views of the Millennium. Therefore, we must conclude that we are now not able to discern the true interpretation of Scripture and that, in God's grace, there will often be more than one interpretation that is responsible, even if none gains the full agreement of all our brothers and sisters in Christ. As a result, while each of us holds a deep conviction concerning our own view, we should do so with grace and with respect for others who hold one of the other two positions.

Speed Bump!

Slow down to be sure you've gotten the main points of this chapter.

Question
Answer

Q1. What is premillennialism?

A1. Premillennialism is the belief that the second coming of Christ will inaugurate a *literal* period of 1,000 years, during which Christ will rule over the world as its political leader.

Q2. What is postmillennialism?

A2. Postmillennialism is the belief that the Gospel will spread throughout the earth creating an increasingly *better* world, after which Jesus returns to bring this age to a close and usher in eternity.

Q3. What is amillennialism?

A3. Amillennialism is the belief that the thousand-year reign of Christ is purely *symbolic* of the ultimate triumph of God's righteousness and goodness in the world.

Fill in the Blank

Question
Answer

Q1. What is premillennialism?

A1. Premillennialism is the belief that the second coming of Christ will inaugurate a _____ period of 1,000 years, during which Christ will rule over the world as its political leader.

Q2. What is postmillennialism?

A2. Postmillennialism is the belief that the Gospel will spread throughout the earth creating an increasingly _____ world, after which Jesus returns to bring this age to a close and usher in eternity.

Q3. What is amillennialism?

A3. Amillennialism is the belief that the thousand-year reign of Christ is purely _____ of the ultimate triumph of God's righteousness and goodness in the world.

For Further Thought and Discussion

1. If you held to a position on the Millennium before reading this chapter, do you still hold to the same position? If yes or no, why?

2. If you did not hold to a position on the Millennium before reading this chapter, which position makes the most sense to you, and why?

3. Regardless of what position you hold, how do you think Christians can keep from making this a divisive issue? Can a church hold to a conviction on the Millennium without its becoming a divisive issue? How?

What If I Don't Believe?

If I don't believe in a Millennium of some kind (one represented by one of the three positions presented in this chapter), I may be in danger of embracing an errant view of Scripture. There is plenty of latitude concerning the Millennium, but one ought to be cautious in moving outside the positions in this chapter. If I believe in one of them, I have the hope that that position brings to me, and I can look forward to the joy of righteousness with Christ. Without that hope, I will live in a bleak world.

For Further Thought and Discussion

1. Scripture
The central passage of Scripture on this subject is important to study and understand:

*   Revelation 20:1–10

2. Books
Two helpful books on this subject are:

Contemporary Options In Eschatology: A Study of the Millennium, Millard Erickson
The Meaning of the Millennium: Four Views, Robert Clouse, ed.

Though the mills of God grind slowly,
  Yet, they grind exceeding small;
Though with patience He stands waiting,
  With exactness grinds He all.
■ **Henry W. Longfellow**

What Final Judgment Awaits Humanity?

The human spirit has an inherent sense of and desire for justice, and when we hear of injustice it assaults our conscience. Unfortunately, examples of injustice in America abound, from the ridiculous to the horrifying. Charles Osgood, of radio's "The Osgood File," reported on his program one day that Chris Hayden had been failing a number of subjects and might have to repeat the seventh grade. His father, Charles, had decided to tutor him. Chris had a study hall at the end of each day that was not doing him any good, so for the next eleven weeks Mr. Hayden took Chris out of study hall and they spent two hours a day at home going over Chris's lessons in science, geography, and part of Homer's *Odyssey*. They made flash cards with science terms on them and charts of Greek gods and goddesses.

Hayden told Chris's teachers what he was doing, and he asked them to let him know if they saw any change in his son's performance. Before long, Chris was bringing home much better scores. Chris not only passed all his subjects but came away with an 85.8 average for the quarter. Good for Chris. But bad for his dad.

School officials had their noses out of joint because Hayden had taken his son out of study hall. That's illegal. They charged him with violating the state's Compulsory School Attendance Laws, and he was convicted. Hayden said he was dumbfounded. Osgood said he was, too!

Ridiculous!!!

In another incident, *Reader's Digest* recounted a Detroit *Free Press* article detailing the chilling account of Leslie Williams, who was first paroled in 1972 after serving one year of potentially five years in prison. He had broken into a store, and a plea bargain had reduced

---

In this chapter we learn that . . .

1. The judgment seat of Christ is the place of reward for those who have accepted God while on earth.
2. Those who have accepted God have already been forgiven for their sins and are now being rewarded for their good deeds and faithful obedience to God.
3. The Great White Throne judgment is the place of judgment for those who have rejected God while on earth.
4. Those who have rejected God are judged on the basis of their unbelief and their thoughts, motives, words, and deeds.

---

the charge to "attempted breaking and entering." On parole, he broke into a home in Wixom where a 15-year-old girl was sleeping, and he tried to choke her. Charged with breaking and entering and assault with intent to commit great bodily harm, he was again allowed to plea bargain, to breaking and entering.

Since Williams was on parole, he should have been returned to prison for the remainder of his previous five-year sentence. Instead, he got a sentence of 18 months to ten years.

After two years he was paroled in July 1975. Within weeks he had abducted a teenager at gunpoint and assaulted her. Williams was sentenced to a reassuring 14 to 25 years. Yet he was paroled again in January 1983. After other arrests, imprisonments, and paroles, he eventually killed four teenagers even as his parole officer was reporting that Williams had "no problems" (February 1994, 36).

Horrifying!!!

We are incensed and outraged by injustice. Something deep within us cries out for justice. Whether it is as minor as someone cutting in line in front of us, or as major as murder, we want justice!

Where does this pervasive, innate longing for justice come from? God is a God of justice (Psalm 33:5), and since we are created in His image, we have an innate longing for justice, even if that longing is skewed because of sin.

Because God is a just God, each person, when he dies, will receive the just reward of his life on earth. But what will those consequences be? The Bible teaches that at the end of the world everyone will be assigned to an eternity united with God or an eternity separated from God. We will all be judged by God at a specific time and place. Those who are united with God will be judged at the judgment seat of Christ. Those who are separated from God will be judged at the Great White Throne judgment. How, then, will we be evaluated, and what will be our reward?

Why I need to know this

I need to know the terrifying consequence of rejecting God and the wonderful consequences of accepting Christ so that I can make a wise decision and help others to make wise decisions regarding their eternal destiny. In addition, having made a wise decision regarding my eternal destiny, I can take joy, hope, and strength from looking forward to my future.

Before we answer those questions, we will remind ourselves that some Christians (mostly amillennialists) believe that these two judgments occur at the same time after the second coming of Christ. Other Christians (mostly premillennialists) believe that the judgment seat of Christ occurs right after the Rapture and before the Great Tribulation, and that the Great White Throne judgment occurs after the Millennium.

What Is the Judgment Seat of Christ?

The judgment seat of Christ is the place of reward for those who have accepted God while on earth.

The phrase "judgment seat of Christ" only occurs twice in the Bible. The first time is in Romans 14:10, where the apostle Paul encourages Christians not to judge each other in matters of legitimate differences of opinion. "But why do you judge your brother? Or why do you show contempt for your brother? For we shall all stand before the judgment seat of Christ." Then in verse 12, we read, "So then, each of us shall give an account of himself to God."

The second passage is 2 Corinthians 5:10, where Paul encourages Christians to live a proper Christian lifestyle. "For we must all appear before the judgment seat of Christ, that each one may receive the things done in the body, according to what he has done, whether good or bad."

The "we" in both passages means *all* Christians. So the judgment seat of Christ is where all Christians will give an account of themselves to God. Because of that, *we* should not judge each other on debatable matters (God will judge us). And *we* should live an exemplary and faithful Christian lifestyle, because we will be held accountable.

The word Paul uses for "judgment seat" is the Greek word *bema*. Outside ancient Corinth in Greece, athletic contests were

Christians will give account of themselves to Jesus before His judgment seat.

held in a large Olympic stadium. When an athlete had won an event, he would come to the judge's bench (*bema*), a raised platform, to receive his reward. This is the sense in which the phrase "judgment seat of Christ" is used. Christians run the race of life (1 Corinthians 9:24; Hebrews 12:1), and when the race is finished they stand before the *bema* on which Christ is seated. We then receive rewards for the quality of our Christian lives on earth. This is not a time of judgment for the unsaved. Only Christians appear here, and there is no punishment meted out. Only rewards. As we will see, some are more greatly rewarded than others, but no one is punished. Christ has already taken the punishment for His children.

On What Basis Are Those Who Have Accepted God Rewarded?

Those who have accepted God have already been forgiven their sins and are now being rewarded for their good deeds and faithful obedience to God.

In 1 Corinthians 3:10–15, we read:

> According to the grace of God which was given to me, as a wise master builder I have laid the foundation, and another builds on it. But let each one take heed how he builds on it. For no other foundation can anyone lay than that which is laid, which is Jesus Christ. Now if anyone builds on this foundation with gold, silver, precious stones, wood, hay, straw, each one's work will become manifest; for the Day will declare it, because it will be revealed by fire; and the fire will test each one's work, of what sort it is. If anyone's work which he has built on it endures, he will receive a reward. If anyone's work is burned, he will suffer loss; but he himself will be saved, yet so as through fire.

The imagery of building a building is used here to depict the ministry. Paul said he had laid the foundation, which was the message of salvation by grace through faith in Jesus Christ. Anyone else who ministers to these new Christians must be sure they build the right kind of building (minister truth properly to these people). After the house is built, a match will be touched to it. This fire is a picture of the judgment of God. If the building is built with gold, silver, and precious stones, the building will not burn, meaning the Christian will receive a reward for ministering truth faithfully to others. If the building is built with wood, hay, and stubble, it will go up in flames because truth was not ministered faithfully to these people.

Those who build the right kind of building will receive rewards.

The word "loss" does not mean the Christian loses salvation, or even that he is punished for building badly. In the imagery, no one beats or kills the builder. The only thing the builder suffers is the loss of his building, the waste of his effort, the loss of profit. But he, himself, will be saved.

It is not difficult to grasp the imagery. Imagine yourself as a builder of residential housing, and you buy a lot for a bargain. Everything about it is good, until you discover that it is in a one-hundred-year flood plain. There is no law against building there, but there is some risk; a bad flood will damage any house built on the lot. A wise builder would not build there. But you decide to risk it. You invest the money and build the house. Afterward, the hundred-year-flood comes and the house is destroyed.

You have not broken any laws. You will not go to jail. But plenty of time, money, and effort are all lost. It was such a waste. The same time and money invested wisely would have yielded a profit.

Some Christians suggest that the judgment seat of Christ will be an ominous day of reckoning for Christians who led careless or rebellious lives. Graham Scroggie, a renowned Bible teacher of a previous generation, wrote, "I would rather go through the Great Tribulation than endure what I believe some Christians will go through at the Judgment Seat of Christ" (*Prophecy Made Plain,* Carl Johnson, 111).

While all the details of the judgment seat of Christ are uncertain, such a statement seems extreme to me. When we received Jesus, we died in Him (Romans 6:8), we were crucified with Him (Galatians 2:20), and we were born again in holiness and righteousness of the truth, in the very likeness of God (Ephesians 4:24). For what sins did Christ die? Some, but not all? Can we make ourselves acceptable to God by our good deeds? 1 John 1:9

says, "If we confess our sins, He is faithful and just to forgive us
our sins and cleanse us from all unrighteousness." Must we receive forgiveness of sins on our deathbed or else suffer for those
sins after we die?

I believe that this line of thinking is an eclipse of grace, a cutting short of the work of Christ. If Jesus did not die for all our
sins, then we are all in big trouble. If Jesus did not die for all of
our sins, what sins would He judge us for at His judgment seat?
Would it be for the big sins like lying, cheating, immorality, or
the little sins like gluttony, pride, anger? Or would it be the sins
we committed since our last confession? Clearly, we would all be
in a lot of trouble.

I believe that the Bible teachers who warn us about being
punished at the judgment seat of Christ do it out of good motives: to encourage us to holy lives here on earth. However, even
a noble motive will not fly when it is anchored to inaccurate doctrine. "There is therefore now no condemnation to those who are
in Christ Jesus," Paul writes in Romans 8:1. Are we saved by the
blood of Christ *plus* a good thumping after we die? Are we saved
by grace through faith in Jesus *plus* a postmortem trip to the
woodshed? Are we saved by grace *plus* an appropriate amount
of pain experienced in heavenly thumbscrews? Or are we saved
by the love, grace, and mercy of God through faith *plus* nothing?
If salvation equals grace "plus anything," then a "work" can
help get us to heaven. Unfortunately, many people believe this
so strongly that they will flog themselves or crawl over stones
until they are bloody. They believe that they can atone for their
sin through their own suffering. Yet the Bible declares that there
is no atonement for sin through human effort of any kind, either
during this life or after. Jesus Christ atoned for our sins through
His death. That is the way. Nothing else.

**The Lord will
chasten, not punish,
Christians in this
life for their sins.**

This does not mean that the Lord will not
chasten us in this life because of our sins, but
that is not punishment. Chastening is meant to
turn us from our sins that we may live in righteousness. Hebrews 12 says, "Therefore we
also, since we are surrounded by so great a cloud of witnesses,
let us lay aside every weight, and the sin which so easily ensnares us, and let us run with endurance the race that is set before us . . ." (verse 1).

If we do, all is well. If we don't, we are chastened by God.

My son, do not despise the chastening of the Lord,
Nor be discouraged when you are rebuked by Him;
For whom the Lord loves He chastens,
And scourges every son whom He receives. . . .

Now no chastening seems to be joyful for the present, but grievous; nevertheless, afterward it yields the peaceable fruit of righteousness to those who have been trained by it (Hebrews 12:5, 11).

Clearly, if we do not lay aside known sin God will chasten us. But He does so in order to train us in righteousness; that is, we must respond properly to it. If we do not, we may receive greater chastening.

The New Testament gives two striking examples of these principles, both in the church at Corinth. In 1 Corinthians 5, a Christian is living in adultery with his stepmother, and the church not only lets it continue but prides itself in its open-mindedness to the situation. Paul says that this is not right. He commands the church to excommunicate the man, to drive him out of the church. In doing this, the church delivers this sinning Christian to Satan for the destruction of the flesh, that his spirit may be saved in the day of the Lord Jesus (verse 5). This is not retribution; it is a desire to get the sinning one to turn from his sin and live in righteousness.

We see the fruit of this undertaking in 2 Corinthians 2:5–9. The man had repented and Paul urged the Corinthian church to forgive him and restore him to fellowship, so that he is not completely overwhelmed by his sorrow.

That is the point of God's chastening, to restore the Christian to righteousness.

But what if the Christian does not repent? Then he receives greater and greater judgment on his sins. In 1 Corinthians 11, some Christians were abusing the Lord's Supper. This was a ceremonial meal in which a small portion of food was eaten, followed by the bread and the cup. Some Christians who had not eaten before they came to this meal stuffed themselves on the ceremonial food and got drunk on the wine, which was a sacrilege. As a result, some of those involved in this sin had become weak, others were sick, and some had even died (verse 30). This latter severe judgment was levied, apparently, because those people refused to repent, and that judgment, apparently, caused others to repent because they had seen the chastening hand of God.

So, flagrant, unrepentant sin by Christians will be chastened in this life by God, but not for retribution. It is to get the sinning Christian to repent and live in righteousness. If he refuses, his life may be taken, which stops the sin and shows others that they cannot trifle with sin and God.

After a Christian dies there is no further opportunity for repentance.

Once that Christian dies, there is no more opportunity to repent and turn from sin. Once a Christian dies, his born-again spirit is united with a redeemed body. There is no more presence of sin and no more desire or even ability to sin. Then, what would be the point of chastening the person? And punishment is out of the question, because Jesus took our punishment for sin. If we have to pay the price, in punishment, for even one sin, that price is eternal condemnation.

In her book *Heaven*, Joni Erickson Tada wrote about her dread of coming before the judgment seat of Christ. She feared that all the bad things she had ever done would be visible to all the other redeemed:

> I saw myself standing under a marquee of a theater: NOW SHOWING, THE UNCENSORED VERSION OF *JONI*. I pictured myself walking down the aisle and [spotting] the handicapped boy in school I made fun of and the girl down the street I beat up in a fistfight. I pictured reaching the first row, sinking into a seat, and cringing as God then rolled the movie of my life for all to gawk at. Talk about guilt and judgment! (57).

In 1 Corinthians 4:5, however, there is a different emphasis: "Therefore judge nothing before the time, until the Lord comes, who will both bring to light the hidden things of darkness and reveal the counsels of the hearts; and then each one's praise will come from God."

Joni then writes:

> Read that one more time. Each will receive his praise from God. When Christ ascends His throne and sits at the judgment seat, I don't believe He'll roll an uncut, uncensored version of your life. He won't wear the scowl of a rigid and inflexible judge who bangs the gavel and reads aloud your sins for the court record. No, that already happened at another judgment. The judgment at the cross. It was there

the Father slammed down the gavel and pronounced His Son "Guilty!" as He became sin for us. It went on record in the courts of heaven and then the indictment was canceled with the words "Paid in Full," written not with red ink, but red blood. Anyway "If you, O Lord, kept a record of sins, O Lord, who could stand? But with you there is forgiveness; therefore you are feared (Psalm 130:3–4, NIV) (*Heaven, Your Real Home,* 58).

The judgment seat of Christ, therefore, is not a place of punishment for Christians. It is not to be feared. It is a place of reward.

What are the rewards which a Christian will receive? Well, we don't know for sure. There are only a few rewards mentioned, and they are not the kinds of rewards we often think of. We think of a bigger mansion to live in, or a better address in the heavenly city, or a higher place in the pecking order of heaven. I wonder if those are adequate concepts of reward.

One picture of rewards is found in 1 Corinthians 3:10–15. We don't know exactly what rewards this passage means, but if we build with symbolic gold, silver, and precious stone—which are word pictures for faithful obedience to God—then we will receive a reward.

Other rewards are called "crowns," and five are mentioned in Scripture. It is not likely that these crowns are literal crowns, but if they are they also represent a larger truth.

1. *The Imperishable Crown* is given to those who run the race of life well, to those who compete according to the rules, and for disciplining the body (1 Corinthians 9:24–27). This crown represents the marvelous truth that nothing God gives to us will ever perish. The crowns given to earthly athletes were made of green leaves that withered shortly after they were received. Never with God! His rewards do not perish, fade, or spoil.
2. *The Crown of Rejoicing* is given to those who have introduced people to Christ (1 Thessalonians 2:19–20). This crown symbolizes that God gives us joy which lasts forever.
3. *The Crown of Righteousness* is given to those who lived in light of the Lord's second coming (2 Timothy 4:8). This crown symbolizes that God will give us sinless perfection, holiness, and a right standing before Him forever. Our struggle with sin will be over forever. Nothing will ever stand between us and God again.

4. *The Crown of Life* is given to those who love the Lord and were faithful to Him (James 1:12, Revelation 2:10). This crown symbolizes that we will live forever in perfect fellowship and harmony with God and with all others of God's children.

5. *The Crown of Glory* is given to those who are faithful in ministering to other Christians (1 Peter 5:1–4). This crown symbolizes that God will shower us with a glory that will never fade. We will be exalted in the halls of heaven, by His grace and love.

Rewards are not meant to encourage a materialistic mindset about heaven. The person who engages in good works in order to get a bigger mansion in heaven and a higher place in the celestial pecking order does not have the right idea about rewards. God offers rewards as a legitimate way of responding to our sincere efforts to serve Him. Yet, even our ability to serve Him is a gift He gives us. Philippians 2:12–13, exhorts us to be faithful and obedient to God because it is God working in us that enables us to serve Him:

> Therefore, my beloved, as you have always obeyed, not as in my presence only but now much more in my absence, work out your own salvation with fear and trembling; for it is God who works in you both to will and to do for his good pleasure."

Even our desires and abilities to serve God are gifts from Him.

All service to God should be motivated by love for Him, not because we will strike heavenly pay dirt.

In addition, the worshipers in Revelation 4 are casting their crowns before the throne, saying, "You are worthy, O Lord, to receive glory and honor and power; for You created all things, and by Your will they exist and were created" (verse 11). If God gives even rewards by His grace, it seems appropriate that we give the crowns back to Him as a gesture of our recognition of His grace.

Just as parents do not want their children to obey them simply to get a bigger allowance, neither does the Lord want us to serve Him merely to hit heavenly pay dirt. The powerful, underlying motive for service to God should be rooted in our relationship with Him; namely, to have Him look at us and hear Him say, "Well done, good and faithful servant. . . . Enter into the joy of your Master" (Matthew 25:23).

What Is the Great White Throne Judgment?

The Great White Throne judgment is the place of judgment for those who have rejected God while on earth.

In sharp contrast to the joyful judgment seat of Christ, an event to reward those who have accepted God, the Great White Throne judgment is an event of dread and punishment for those who have rejected God. Hebrews 9:27 states, ". . . it is appointed for men to die once, but after this the judgment . . ." Psalm 9:7–8 reads, "He has prepared His throne for judgment. He shall judge the world in righteousness . . ."

The central Biblical passage on the Great White Throne is Revelation 20:10–11:

> Then I saw a great white throne and Him who sat on it, from whose face the earth and the heaven fled away. And there was found no place for them. And I saw the dead, small and great, standing before God and books were opened. And another book was opened, which is the Book of Life. And the dead were judged according to their works, by the things which were written in the books.

From this and other passages we learn several key things about this terrifying event.

The Judge Is Jesus

From the Revelation passage we learn that there is a judge, but it does not say who the judge is. The writings of the apostle John, however, reveal that the judge is Jesus:

> For the Father judges no one, but has committed all judgment to the Son, that all should honor the Son just as they honor the Father. For as the Father has life in Himself, so He has granted the Son to have life in Himself, and has given Him authority to execute judgment also, because He is the Son of Man. (John 5:22, 26, 27)

The apostle Paul supported this:

> God told us to announce clearly to the people that Jesus is the one he has chosen to judge the living and the dead. (Acts 10:42)
> He has set a day when he will judge the world's people with fairness. And he has chosen the man Jesus to do the judging for him. (Acts 17:31)
> When Christ Jesus comes as king, he will be the judge of every-

one, whether they are living or dead. (2 Timothy 4:1, *Contemporary English Version*.)

Those who have rejected God throughout history will stand before Jesus at the Great White Throne.

Clearly, Jesus is the judge at the Great White Throne judgment. Jesus will be on the Great White Throne. His presence at the judgment seat of Christ as righteous Savior is a source of comfort. His presence at the Great White Throne judgment as righteous judge is a source of terror.

Those Judged Are Unbelievers

Those people who are judged at the Great White Throne judgment have rejected God throughout history, from Adam's son Cain, who killed his brother, to those who rebelled during the end of the Millennium and are killed at the second coming of Christ. In Revelation 20:12–13, we read, "And I saw the dead, small and great, standing before God. . . . The sea gave up the dead who were in it, and Death and Hades delivered up the dead who were in them."

From this and the previous passages, we see that all who reject God, from the first unbeliever to the last, will stand before Jesus at the Great White Throne.

On What Basis Are Those Who Have Rejected God Judged for Sin?

Those who have rejected God are judged on the basis of their unbelief and their thoughts, motives, words, and deeds.

When the unbelieving stand before Jesus at the Great White Throne, it will not be a trial to determine guilt or innocence. That has already been determined. They are there because they are guilty. But of what are they guilty? John 3:18 tells us, "He who believes in Him [Jesus] is not condemned; but he who does not believe is condemned already, because he has not believed in the name of the only begotten Son of God."

Many people think that the unsaved are judged because their bad works outweigh their good works. This is a big mistake. If we were judged as "saved" or "unsaved" based on our works, all of us would be lost (Romans 3:23; 6:23). Instead, people are lost because they rejected what they knew about God, either from creation or from the Bible (Romans 1:18–21). This does not necessarily mean they were not religious. Pastors, priests, bishops, Christian workers, and faithful followers of religion from all times and places will be at the Great White Throne judgment. However, in their heart they did not accept God as their Savior and Lord.

Even though everyone who is lost is lost because they did not respond fully to the true light that is available to everyone ever born (John 1:9), there appear to be degrees of punishment of unbelievers based on the quality of their lives. Those who were kind and good will be judged less severely than those who were cruel and evil. We see this idea established in Revelation 20:12. "And I saw the dead, small and great, standing before God, and books were opened. And another book was opened, which is the Book of Life. And the dead were judged according to their works, by the things which were written in the books."

In addition, Jesus said in Matthew 11:22–24, regarding some cities that had rejected Him:

> **People will be lost because they did not fully respond to true light.**

> But I say to you, it will be more tolerable for Tyre and Sidon in the day of judgment than for you. And you, Capernaum, who are exalted to heaven, will be brought down to Hades; for if the mighty works which were done in you had been done in Sodom, it would have remained until this day. But I say to you that it shall be more tolerable for the land of Sodom in the day of judgment than for you.

In Luke 12:47–48, we read:

> And that servant who knew his master's will, and did not prepare himself or do according to his will, shall be beaten with many stripes. But he who did not know, yet committed things worthy of stripes, shall be beaten with few. For everyone to whom much is given, from him much will be required; and to whom much has been committed, of him they will ask the more.

It seems evident, then, that different degrees of punishment await those who are unsaved, punishment based on their thoughts, motives, words, and deeds here on earth.

Concerning thoughts and motives, we find in Hebrews 4:12–13 that the word of God is able to "discern the thoughts and intents of the heart," and that "all things are naked and open to the eyes of Him to whom we must give an account."

Concerning our words, Matthew 12:36–37 reads, "But I say to you that for every idle word men may speak, they will give account of it in the day of judgment. For by your words you will be justified, and by your words you will be condemned."

Concerning our actions, Revelation 20:13 states that "the dead were judged according to their works."

Therefore, we see the need for justice satisfied, in that all people will receive eternal reward either for their own righteousness or for Jesus'. We either stand before the judgment seat of Christ in His merit, or we stand before the Great White Throne in our own merit. At the former we receive reward. At the latter, we receive judgment.

Conclusion

Our longing for justice reflects our having been created in God's image. As we long for justice on earth, so He longs for justice in heaven. A day will come when both the righteous (in Christ) and the unrighteous (out of Christ) will get what they deserve. At the judgment seat of Christ, those in Christ receive the just rewards of having righteousness in Him. At the Great White Throne judgment, those who have rejected God receive the just rewards of their unbelief and sin. In both places, one delightful, the other terrifying, justice will be served.

Speed Bump!

Slow down to be sure you've gotten the main points of this chapter.

Question Answer

Q1. What is the judgment seat of Christ?

A1. The judgment seat of Christ is the place of *reward* for those who have accepted God while on earth.

Q2. On what basis are those who have accepted God rewarded?

A2. Those who have accepted God have already been forgiven for their sins and are now being rewarded for their good deeds and faithful *obedience* to God.

Q3. What is the Great White Throne judgment?

A3. The Great White Throne judgment is the place of *judgment* for those who have rejected God while on earth.

Q4. On what basis are those who have rejected God judged for sin?

A4. Those who have rejected God are judged on the basis of their *unbelief* and their thoughts, motives, words, and deeds.

Fill in the Blank

Question Answer

Q1. What is the judgment seat of Christ?

A1. The judgment seat of Christ is the place of _____ for those who have accepted God while on earth.

Q2. On what basis are those who have accepted God rewarded?

A2. Those who have accepted God have already been forgiven for their sins and are now being rewarded for their good deeds and faithful _____ to God.

Q3. What is the Great White Throne judgment?

A3. The Great White Throne judgment is the place of _____ for those who have rejected God while on earth.

Q4. On what basis are those who have rejected God judged for sin?

A4. Those who have rejected God are judged on the basis of their _____ and their thoughts, motives, words, and deeds.

For Further Thought and Discussion

1. If you are a Christian, describe the role that a fear of punishment played in your decision to become a Christian.

2. If you are not yet a Christian, what role does a fear of punishment play in your evaluation of whether or not to become a Christian?

3. If you are a Christian, describe the role that a desire for reward played in your decision to become a Christian.

4. If you are not yet a Christian, what role does a desire for eternal reward play in your evaluation to become a Christian?

What If I Don't Believe?

If I don't believe in judgment for unbelief and sin, I might underestimate the negative consequences of rejecting God and place myself in dire eternal peril. If I don't believe in reward for faith and obedience, I may not have adequate motivation for faith and obedience, and I may not draw enough hope and encouragement from the future for getting through the trials of today.

For Further Study

1. Scripture
There are several important passages of Scripture to study concerning this subject. They include:

- 1 Corinthians 3:10–15

- Hebrews 12:5–11

- Philippians 2:12–13

- Revelation 20:10–15

- John 5:22, 26, 27

2. Books
There are several other books which are helpful in studying this subject further.

Knowing God (Chapters 14–17), James I. Packer
Contemporary Options in Eschatology, Millard Erickson

Has this world been so kind to you that you would leave it with regret? There are better things ahead than any we leave behind.
■ **C.S. Lewis**

8

What Is Death?

On a medical or scientific level, death is a profound mystery. Dr. Maurice Rawlings, a cardiologist, writes:

> The face was bloated and blue when the dead body arrived, eyes bulging, tongue protruding between swollen lips. Way too late for Heimlich maneuvers or CPR. I found an unchewed piece of steak in his windpipe. Probably suffocation from an obstructed airway, but an unwitnessed departure of life at age thirty-four always requires an autopsy. We called the pathologist and cut the body open.
>
> What is this death we see every day? The old cliché applies, I suppose—the body dies when the spirit leaves it. But what really happens at death? One moment we're animated and moving about. The next moment nothing, and the animation is gone (*To Hell and Back* 1).

Yes, death is a mystery, even to those who see it regularly. Is it that the body dies because the spirit leaves it, as Rawlings speculates? Or is it that the spirit leaves when the body dies? And when the spirit is separated from a dead body, what happens to the spirit?

For certain, death is a foreboding mystery. "I'm tired of living, but scared of dying," is a line from the old song "Old Man River" that just about sums it up. Sooner or later, many people get tired of living but are scared of dying. Because of personal pain or boredom or old age, life itself can become a chore, yet we are intimidated by dying.

In this chapter we learn that . . .

1. When a person dies, his physical body ceases to function and his spirit departs to the spiritual realm for his eternal destiny.
2. The intermediate state refers to human existence in the interval between a person's death and his resurrection to heaven or hell.
3. Everyone is resurrected from physical death, some to heaven and others to hell.

Even the efforts of poets and philosophers to reduce death's intimidation usually end up as just so much "whistling in the dark," pretending that there is nothing to fear from death, in the hope that "wishing will make it so."

William Cullen Bryant writes in *Thanatopsis:*

> So live, that when thy summons comes to join
> The innumerable caravan which moves
> To that mysterious realm, where each shall take
> His chamber in the silent halls of death,
> Thou go not, like the quarry-slave at night,
> Scourged to his dungeon, but, sustained and soothed
> By an unfaltering trust, approach thy grave,
> Like one that wraps the drapery of his couch
> About him, and lies down to pleasant dreams.

Fine! *If* there is no hell! But if there is a hell, where does the "sustained," "soothed," "unfaltering trust" come from? Who so easily gives out advice for meeting the great unwanted and unanswered experience of life? How does Bryant know that "pleasant dreams" will not be a nightmare? On what authority does this poet write his opinion? What if he's wrong?

Bryant is not alone. Shakespeare whistled a little in *Julius Caesar:*

> It seems to me most strange that men should fear;
> Seeing that death, a necessary end,
> Will come when it will come.

Well, that's okay, if death is the permanent cessation of "being" and consciousness. But what if death is simply the doorway into another realm of existence? What then, Shakespeare?

Francis Bacon wrote that "men fear death as children fear to go in the dark; and as that natural fear in children is increased with tales, so is the other." True, perhaps. But what if the tales are true? Whistle on, Mr. Bacon.

Dylan Thomas wrote the bold words:

> Do not go gentle into that good night . . .
> Rage, rage against the dying of the light.

But what good would that do? So you rage? How has that made anything different after your last breath?

The ultimate example of whistling in the dark is the poem *Invictus,* by William Earnest Henley:

Out of the night that covers me,
  Black as the Pit from pole to pole,
I thank what ever gods may be
  For my unconquerable soul.

In the fell clutch of circumstance,
  I have not winced nor cried aloud;
Under the bludgeonings of chance
  My head is bloody, but unbowed.

It matters not how straight the gate,
  How charged with punishment the scroll.
I am the master of my fate,
  I am the captain of my soul.

This is one of the most absurd statements I have ever heard. Not yet a Christian, I read it in high school, and even then I thought, *just let God get His hands on you, and you'll whistle another tune. You are not the master of your fate. You are not the captain of your soul. Death is beyond you. If there is not a God, you will cease to be, in which case you were not a captain or a master. You simply floated down the stream of life like a cork, and in the end, got annihilated. You were lucky. And if there is a God, you are not a captain or master. You will meet the Captain and Master, and take orders from Him.*

Why I need to know this

I need to know what happens when I die so that I can adequately prepare myself for it. The one certainty in life is death, and if there is anything I can do before I die to make it safe to die, that would be my number-one priority in life.

I am an expert at fearing death. I feared death all my life. I will never forget lying in bed one night trying to go to sleep when I was twelve, thinking, *twelve years old! It seems that just yesterday I was six! I'm going to die!* So I have always been keenly interested in anyone's statements about death. However, I was not very old before I realized that what people said about death was worthless unless God said the same thing. Who were they to make authoritative statements about death? Maybe they were like the blind leading the blind.

Of more comfort to me were Tennyson's words in *Crossing the Bar:*

Sunset and evening star,
   And one clear call for me!
And may there be no moaning of the bar,
   When I put out to sea,

But such a tide as moving seems asleep,
   Too full for sound and foam,
When that which drew from out the boundless deep
   Turns again home.

Twilight and evening bell,
   And after that the dark!
And may there be no sadness of farewell,
   When I embark;

For though from out our bourne of Time and Place
   The flood may bear me far,
I hope to see my Pilot face to face
   When I have crossed the bar.

Though I was then ignorant, I too hoped that somehow, some-way, someday, I would meet my Pilot face to face when I died and "crossed the bar."

Then through God's grace the gospel came to me and I believed. I no longer fear death as I did, and I am so glad that as a child I put no confidence in the declarations of men and women. I knew that if anything "safe" was to be believed about death, it had to come from God. So, what does God say about death?

What Happens When a Person Dies?

When a person dies, his physical body ceases to function and his spirit departs to the spiritual realm for his eternal destiny.

Many years ago, we used to believe that a person died when he stopped breathing. Then our understanding of the human body progressed and we believed that a person died, not when he stopped breathing, but when the heart stopped beating. Then we believed that death occurred when brain waves on an EEG went flat. Today we know that people have been resuscitated from no breathing, no heart beat, and flat brain waves. In fact, people who have drowned by falling through the ice, and who have been submerged and "dead" for hours, have been resuscitated. Their body temperature was lowered so dramatically from the icy water that normal physical deterioration did not occur.

There are also the strange accounts of people's spirits seemingly leaving their bodies, in what have become known as near-death experiences (NDEs). These are mysterious indeed, but so many have been reported that it causes one to wonder. Dr. Maurice Rawlings is perhaps the most believable evangelical Christian to compile evidence on such experiences. He has written about them in two best-selling books, *Beyond Death's Door* and *To Hell and Back.* In one example, a lady recounted:

Over the years there have been many theories about when death occurs.

> My temperature was almost 106 and I was having cardiac arrhythmias. I felt an incredible pain. The wall of my uterus was ripping apart. I was in septic shock, going into labor. As I lost consciousness I heard a voice shouting, "I can't get her blood pressure!"
>
> And then within the tiniest fraction of an instant, I was out of my body and out of pain. I was up on the ceiling in a corner of the room, looking down, watching doctors and nurses rush around frantically as they worked to save my life (*To Hell and Back* 33).

This is a typical "happening" that is reported in these kinds of events. In another example, during a battle in Vietnam, Captain Tommy Clack had an explosive hit him in the foot:

> I was immediately thrown into the air, and when I landed on the ground, I sat up and realized that my legs, my right arm and my right shoulder were gone. . . . All of a sudden I was out of my body, looking at them working on me, and then they covered me with a poncho, indicative of death. We arrived at a MASH unit, and I was taken into an operating room. I watched them cut off my uniform, and at this point a massive bright light permeated the room. It was a wonderful, warm, good thing, like looking into the sun. Then . . . I was back out at the battlefield. Around me were people I had served with who had died. . . . They tried to get me to go with them, but I would not go. Then, in the blink of an eye, I was back in the operating room, watching the scenario (37–38).

Stories like these used to be discounted as mere hallucinations. In many instances, however, people having "out-of-body" experiences (OBEs) know and observe things that they could not possibly have known or observed if they had been confined strictly to the hospital bed. So it is unlikely that they are hallucinating. Whatever is happening in such cases, it certainly transcends our standard understanding of death and of separation of spirit from body, and of what happens when one dies.

When a person dies, the spirit departs the body and awaits its eternal destiny.

However, all people, even those fortunate to return from an OBE or an NDE, inevitably die; the spirit leaves the body, never to return. This is death as we understand it from the Bible. Hebrews 9:27 says, "It is appointed for men to die once, but after this the judgment." So, apparently, we cannot die more than once in the biblical sense. The out-of-body and near-death experiences do not qualify as death. When a person dies in the biblical sense there is no coming back. The body stops functioning and the spirit departs to the spiritual realm for its eternal destiny.

What Is the Intermediate State?

The intermediate state refers to human existence in the interval between an individual's death and his resurrection to heaven or hell.

We are now moving into deep water because, though the Bible is not entirely silent about this interval, the subject leaves so many questions unanswered. So we will investigate what we do know, while being cautious about what we don't.

Millions of people have died since Abel, and many millions, or billions, may die before Jesus returns. What happens to us between the time we die and the time we receive a resurrected body? Do we float around the heavens as disembodied spirits? Do we get a temporary body? Where do we spend our time? In heaven, in hell, or in a "holding tank"? In other words, what is our intermediate state like?

The Bible is not crystal clear, but it does provide some insight.

Old Testament

The Old Testament speaks of a shadowy place called "Sheol," which is usually translated as "the grave," although it is not often clear even what that means. It refers to the realm of both the righteous and unrighteous dead. The wicked enter there at death (Job 21:13), the righteous are ultimately saved from it (Psalm 49:15). It has no lasting hold on the righteous because

God will ransom them from its power (Hosea 13:14), and God does not abandon the righteous to Sheol (Psalm 16:10). Exactly what that means is not clear. In the *Evangelical Dictionary of Theology,* we read:

> Both the righteous and the wicked go to Sheol. When the righteous go to the grave (Sheol) they are delivered from it, whereas the wicked remain there (grave or hell). Because relevant Scriptures seem to teach a marked difference between the ultimate end of the wicked and righteous with respect to Sheol, one might assert that the Old Testament supports neither a general view of an underworld where all souls go nor a soul sleep of the wicked [soul sleep will be discussed later].

New Testament

Both the first-century Jews and the early Christians held the abode of the dead to be a highly compartmentalized place that separated the righteous and the unrighteous. In Luke 16:19–31, a beggar named Lazarus dies and goes to "Abraham's bosom" and a rich man dies and goes to "Hades." The former is a place of comfort; the latter, a place of torment. The two places are separated by a "great gulf" so that people in one place cannot get to the other place. It is hotly debated as to whether this is to be understood literally or symbolically, but in either interpretation the dead go to a realm that appears to have one place for the unrighteous dead and another place for the righteous dead.

When Jesus was being crucified with the two criminals, one of them said mockingly, "If you are the Christ, save Yourself and us" (Luke 23:39). But the other one said, "Lord, remember me when You come into Your kingdom" (verse 42). To that one, Jesus replied, "Assuredly, I say to you, today you will be with Me in Paradise" (verse 43). The assumption among most Bible scholars is that "Paradise" means the place where the beggar Lazarus went in Luke 16.

Another view called "soul sleep" has persisted throughout church history. This means that when believers die they go into a state of unconscious existence, and that the next thing they are conscious of will be when Christ returns, raises them to eternal life, and gives them their resurrection bodies. This view has never been widely held, but it is based on the following two points. First, the Bible speaks of death as "sleep," and, second, if we don't get our resurrection bodies until Christ comes back (an assumption within this view) then it seems logical that we simply "sleep" between the time of death and bodily resurrection.

However, when the Bible speaks of "sleep" it often is a metaphor for death. It suggests that as sleep is temporary, so physical death is temporary. We all awake from sleep to begin life again the next day, and all who die will awake from physical death.

This metaphorical use is seen, for example, when Jesus spoke about the death of his friend Lazarus (not the beggar). He said, "Our friend Lazarus sleeps, but I go that I may wake him up" (John 11:11). His disciples completely misunderstand and suggest that if Lazarus is only asleep he will wake up. When they wonder what the big deal is, Jesus said it plainly, "Lazarus is dead" (verse 14). And to the one believing criminal on the cross, Jesus said, ". . . today you will be with Me in Paradise" (Luke 23:43). If the criminal went into soul sleep, there is no apparent way that he could be with Jesus in Paradise.

"Sleep" in the Bible is often a metaphor for a believer's death.

Other passages give little room for the concept of soul sleep. In Philippians 1:23, where Paul says, "I am hard pressed . . . , having a desire to depart and be with Christ . . . ," and 2 Corinthians 5:8, "We are confident, yes, well pleased rather to be absent from the body and to be present with the Lord." One cannot be slumbering unconsciously and be "with Christ" at the same time.

One valid question, however, is raised by the question of soul sleep. If we do not sleep until the Resurrection, and if we do not get our eternal bodies until the Resurrection, then in what state does our spirit exist between physical death and resurrection? Are we spirit beings without bodies? That is not inconceivable, since God is spirit and is able to relate to others "in spirit." Or do we get a temporary, intermediate body that will be replaced with a permanent body at the final Resurrection? That is what I was taught in seminary. The view is based on the observation that we have bodies on earth and bodies in eternity, so consistency suggests some kind of body between our physical death and resurrection. But there is no hard biblical evidence for either position.

Who Is Resurrected from Physical Death?

Everyone is resurrected from physical death, some to heaven and others to hell.

While the timing is debated among Christians, the fact of resurrection is not. Revelation 20:13–15 makes it terrifyingly clear that the unrighteous are resurrected:

> The sea gave up the dead who were in it, and Death and Hades delivered up the dead who were in them. And they were judged, each one according to his works. Then Death and Hades were cast into the lake of fire. This is the second death. And anyone not found written in the Book of Life was cast into the lake of fire.

We know little about the resurrection bodies of the unsaved, but the chilling picture of this passage makes the nature of the bodies incidental to the terror that those bodies will experience because of their sin.

In startling and wonderful contrast, 1 Corinthians 15:51–54 says:

> Behold, I tell you a mystery: We shall not all sleep, but we shall all be changed—in a moment, in the twinkling of an eye, at the last trumpet. For the trumpet will sound, and the dead will be raised incorruptible, and we shall be changed. For this corruptible must put on incorruption, and this mortal must put on immortality. So when this corruptible has put on incorruption, and this mortal has put on immortality, then shall be brought to pass the saying that is written: "Death is swallowed up in victory."

Physical resurrection is not simply the eternal extension of life as it is now known, but a new kind of existence. If our resurrection bodies are like Jesus' resurrection body, and we assume they will be (1 Corinthians 15:1–58), then our bodies will be marvelous indeed. Jesus in His Resurrection body, was able **Physical resurrection means a new kind of life.** to appear and disappear at will, passing through walls and doors as though they were not there (John 20:19–29). We will experience no more death or pain (Revelation 21:4). Presumably, we will be able to travel at the speed of thought, since the speed of light would be much too slow to be able to get around in the universe. It would take 100,000 light-years just to travel from one side of our Milky Way galaxy to the other, and there are 100 billion galaxies that we know of. It is doubtful that Jesus would be limited to such unacceptably slow means of travel, and if our bodies are of the same kind as Jesus', neither would we. We will live forever, unimpeded in any way by sin, and it will be marvelous indeed.

Conclusion

When I became a Christian, it was a great relief to get free of the fear of death, which had seemed like a big, yawning black hole into which people dropped to unknown consequences. This terrified me. Then, I became a Christian in the mid-1960s, during a time of intense interest in prophecy. After hearing sermons and reading books about the signs of the times, I became convinced that I would not have to die. The Lord would come back first. This was an even greater relief to me.

Now, thirty years later, I am less persuaded that I will not die. In fact, I have faced the real possibility that I will. But one thing is different. While I am not eager to face the dying process, which could include accident, disease, and pain, I no longer fear death. I welcome it. I am no longer disconcerted by it, as I was when I first became a Christian. I see it as a door opening from one room of my life into a far better one.

But many people are squarely where I was in the early days of my Christian experience and even before, when I feared death greatly. It is not uncommon for Christians to ask why they have to die. Is death a punishment for Christians? No, Romans 8:1 explains that there is no condemnation to those who are in Christ Jesus, because all the penalties for our sins have been paid by Jesus.

Physical death is merely the final outcome of living in a fallen world, for when Adam and Eve ate from the forbidden tree sin entered the world, and along with it both spiritual and physical death. But just as a kernel of wheat falls to the ground and dies, Jesus said, so it will sprout again into new life. We must die so that sin can be eradicated, and we can be physically born again to new life, just as we have been spiritually. It is through death that we are finally completed in our union with

Christ (Romans 8:22–23). Physical death is a wonderful gift. Without it, we would have to live eternally in sin-corrupted bodies. So, regardless of what causes our death, the actual process of dying is the closing of our eyes in this world and a moment later opening them in that far, far better world; a world where all that is not good is excluded and all that is good is included, and where we will live with our Lord forever. No problem with that!

Speed Bump!

Slow down to be sure you've gotten the main points from this chapter.

Question
Answer

Q1. What happens when a person dies?

A1. When a person dies, his physical body ceases to function and his spirit *departs* to the spiritual realm for his eternal destiny.

Q2. What is the intermediate state?

A2. The intermediate state refers to human existence in the *interval* between a person's death and his resurrection to heaven or hell.

Q3. Who is resurrected from physical death?

A3. *Everyone* is resurrected from physical death, some to heaven and others to hell.

Fill in the Blanks

Question
Answer

Q1. What happens when a person dies?

A1. When a person dies, his physical body ceases to function and his spirit _____ to the spiritual realm for his eternal destiny.

Q2. What is the intermediate state?

A2. The intermediate state refers to human existence in the _____ between a person's death and his resurrection to heaven or hell.

Q3. Who is resurrected from physical death?

A3. _____ is resurrected from physical death, some to heaven and others to hell.

For Further Thought and Discussion

1. Have you thought much about your own death? Does the thought frighten you? Are you ready to die? Do you think you will die, or do you think the Lord will return first?

2. Do you believe that at your physical death, your spirit lives on? If you are not ready to die, what do you need to do to become ready?

What If I Don't Believe?

If I don't believe that my spirit lives on after death and is assigned to either heaven or hell, then I am rejecting one of the fundamentals of the Christian faith. I am taking the greatest risk any human can take. If I reject the teachings of the Bible, and if I reject God, I am betting my eternal destiny that there is no God, or that He would not send me to hell for rejecting Him. I am playing Russian Roulette.

For Further Study

1. Scripture
There are several passages of Scripture that are helpful in studying this subject:

*   Hebrews 9:27

*   Revelation 20:13–15

*   1 Corinthians 15:51–54

2. Books
There are other books which are helpful in studying this subject further. They include:

Immortality—The Other Side of Death, Gary R. Habermas and J.P. Moreland
Before Death Comes, Maurice Rawlings
Life, Death and Beyond, J. Kerby Anderson
Deceived by the Light, Douglas Groothuis

The safest road to hell is the gradual one—the gentle slope, soft underfoot, without sudden turnings, without milestones, without signposts.
C.S. Lewis

9

What Is Hell?

I cannot remember ever disbelieving in hell. Hell, in fact, troubled me greatly, and it had a direct bearing on my becoming a Christian. I didn't want to go there, so I was willing to do whatever I needed to do to avoid it.

As a young child I would gaze into the hottest coals of a campfire at night and imagine it as a miniature picture of hell. Inside the unburned outer logs, inside the flaming edges, inside the hottest coals was a near white-hot center that made my face burn from several feet away. While I do not recommend it, I dropped a bug into that small inferno out of intense curiosity; it writhed in agony for a moment and was immediately consumed. I gaped. I couldn't imagine that destiny. But suddenly I realized it would be worse than that. *Anyone going to hell*, I thought, *would writhe in agony in the white-hot center of the great Eternal Campfire but never be consumed.* My mind drew back. It was unthinkable.

In this chapter we learn that . . .

1. Hell is eternal separation from God and all that is good.
2. Literalists believe that hell is a place of endless, conscious, physical, spiritual, and emotional suffering in literal fire for those who have rejected God in their earthly life.
3. Metaphoricalists believe that hell is a place of endless, conscious, emotional, and spiritual suffering for those who have rejected God in their earthly life.
4. Conditionalists believe that hell is a place of conscious suffering for those who have rejected God in their earthly life, but which eventually ends.

Another experience fueled my aversion to hell. One time when I was about six, I visited my grandparents' home, and there was a variety show on television. On the stage, a man was dressed like that caricature of the devil, red tights, horns, pitchfork, and tail, and with him were a dozen women dressed like devilettes. As the music played, they all danced, swirled, and pranced around a bunch of little three-foot high volcanoes with dry-ice fog spewing out of them.

I don't remember being frightened by the program, but that evening I had a nightmare. I was in hell, which was like that stage on television. I was hiding behind one of the little volcanoes and the devil and devilettes were swirling around and around looking for me. They finally found me, grabbed me, strapped me to an ironing board and started ironing me!

It's funny now, but I didn't laugh then! In fact, I had that dream on a recurring basis. Even when I became an adult I occasionally woke from that dream terrified. But I have not had that dream since the day I accepted Christ as Lord of my life.

I realize that my images of hell were not exactly biblical. But one thing has stuck with me: even if my imagery was wrong, hell was still to be feared and avoided.

If human mental images of hell are not always accurate, what does the Bible say about hell? Answering that is not always easy. There are different interpretations of hell even among those who believe the Bible is inspired and who hold to all the crucial doctrines of Christianity, such as the deity of Christ, the personality of the Holy Spirit, the lostness of humanity, salvation by grace through faith in Jesus, and that Jesus is coming again. Nevertheless, we begin by looking at three key views.

What Is the Consensus View on Hell?

Hell is eternal separation from God and all that is good.

No matter what a person understands the specifics of hell to be, we know from the Bible that it is always described in ominous and foreboding terms as a place of torment to be avoided at all costs. Today, of course, the concept of hell has fallen by the wayside among those who do not believe in a literal hell. And it is often an awkward subject among those who do believe in a literal hell. So we do not hear much about hell from anyone these days.

To many people, hell is a chilling and unacceptable idea. Sir Arthur Conan Doyle, author of the Sherlock Holmes novels, was

Why I need to know this

I need to know this because I need to be clear that hell, according to the Bible, is a terrible end, and that I must not only be sure to avoid it myself, but I must warn others of it also.

reported to have written that "this odious conception, so blasphemous in its view of the Creator, may perhaps have been of service in a coarse age when men were frightened by fires, as wild beasts are scared by the travelers. Hell as a permanent place does not exist" (*The Other Side of the Good News,* Larry Dixon 19).

Theologians also choke on the bone of hell. Some are doing away with hell, at least in their own minds, others are revising traditional views, and others are ignoring it altogether. Among those who are doing away with hell, Dixon writes:

> Nels Ferré, a professor of theology, said that "*no* worthy faith can ever attribute eternal hell to God. . . . To attribute eternal hell to God is literally blasphemy, the attributing of the worst to the best. From such blasphemy may God deliver everyone." One liberal theologian asks: "Is it possible that any human being can practically believe such a horrible collection of revolting absurdities to be the truth sent us by a loving and merciful God?"
>
> Other theologians also claim that the church suffers at the hand of its speculators. "Hell is only a figment of the theological imagination," said one commentator. Reinhold Niebuhr was dispensing his best advice, some would say, when he stated that "it is unwise for Christians to claim any knowledge of either the furniture of heaven or the temperature of hell" (Dixon 19–20).

Others are revising the traditional concepts, suggesting that there is no literal fire, as has been traditionally held; others are suggesting that hell is a temporary place, or that everyone will eventually be saved from hell.

Among those who still hold to the traditional understanding of hell, few spend much time preaching or teaching about it.

If we are all dead honest with ourselves, perhaps we all find the topic so revolting that we would rather not think about it. C.S. Lewis once wrote, "There is no doctrine which I would more willingly remove from Christianity than [hell], if it lay in my power . . . I would pay any price to be able to say truthfully: 'All will be saved.' "

In spite of all this, we still must find ways to deal credibly with what the Bible says about hell. We must explain the "offending passages" in a way that is consistent with the rest of Scripture, taking into consideration the historic Christian faith. Since it is the position of this book series that the Bible is the ver-

Hell must be explained in a way that preserves the integrity of Scripture.

bally inspired Word of God, we cannot proclaim, willy-nilly, that hell doesn't exist, as liberal theologians sometimes do. We must explain hell in a way that preserves the integrity of the Bible as the Word of God.

Within all the possible interpretations of hell among those who hold a high view of Scripture, is the belief that hell is a place of eternal separation from God, that it is a place of torment, and that it is a place which the Bible warns us to avoid by accepting Jesus as our personal Savior. Beyond this basic "consensus" view there are three major interpretations on hell: the literal view, the metaphorical view, and the conditional view.

What Is the Literal View on Hell?

Literalists believe that hell is a place of endless, conscious, physical, spiritual, and emotional suffering in literal fire for those who have rejected God in their earthly life.

The word translated *hell* in the New Testament comes from the Greek word "Gehenna," which is derived from the valley of Hinnom, located just south of Jerusalem. This place was a city garbage dump that smoldered and burned twenty-four hours a day every day. In this dreadful place, human sacrifices were once offered to the god Molech (2 Kings 23:10), and it was once used as a burial place for criminals. It's not difficult to see why it evolved into a metaphor for the everlasting state of the unsaved.

A number of Bible passages apparently speak of hell as a real place of torment for unbelievers who have died:

- In Matthew 10:28, believers in Christ are told not to be afraid of those who kill the body, but rather to "fear Him who is able to destroy both soul and body in hell."
- In Matthew 7:23, those who are not true converts of Christ, yet who claim to be true converts, will one day be told by Christ, "I never knew you; depart from Me, you who practice lawlessness."

- In Matthew 25:14–30, a devious servant is thrown "into the outer darkness. There will be weeping and gnashing of teeth."
- In Luke 12:47–48 and Mark 12:40, we learn that there may be degrees of punishment in hell; one servant receives a lighter beating than another servant, and evil hypocrites are worthy of greater condemnation than others.
- The apostle Paul describes the punishment of the unbelieving as "sudden destruction" when the Day of the Lord comes (1 Thessalonians 5:3) and they will suffer divine wrath (1 Thessalonians 5:9). The punishment of the unbelieving is described as "everlasting destruction" (2 Thessalonians 1:9). In Hebrews 6:2, "eternal judgment" is prophesied for the unbelieving, and in 10:27, this is enlarged with a reference to a "fearful expectation of judgment, and fiery indignation which will devour the adversaries."

Other passages seem to suggest that this torment is conscious and everlasting:

- If anyone worships the beast, "he shall be tormented with fire and brimstone in the presence of the holy angels and in the presence of the Lamb. And the smoke of their torment ascends forever and ever; and they have no rest day or night . . ." (Revelation 14:10–11).
- And the devil himself, who deceived people will be "cast into the lake of fire and brimstone where the beast and the false prophet are. And they will be tormented day and night forever and ever" (Revelation 20:10).

Of course, a deeply troubling aspect of these passages is that it is difficult to harmonize eternal punishment with the character of God. The popular question is, How can a loving God punish people in unspeakable agony forever? In response to this, John Walvoord writes:

It is difficult to harmonize eternal punishment with the love of God.

> If the slightest sin is infinite in its significance, then it also demands infinite punishment as a divine judgment. Though it is common for all Christians to wish that there were some way out of the doctrine of eternal punishment because of its inexorable and unyielding revelation of divine judgment, one must rely on Christian faith on the doctrine that God is a God of infinite righteousness as

well as infinite love. While on the one hand he bestows infinite grace on those who trust him, he must, on the other hand, inflict eternal punishment on those who spurn him (*Four Views of Hell* 27).

Others see the agonies of hell as more self-inflicted by the unbelieving. If someone will not accept God, then he, by default, chooses the opposite of God. If he will not go to heaven, he gets the opposite of heaven. The opposite of God and heaven (love, joy, peace) is hell (hate, pain, suffering). Someone has said that the gates of hell are locked not from the outside but from the inside.

Sensitive literalists struggle with this grave truth. Yet because they believe in the authenticity and authority of the Scripture, they feel that they have no alternative but to believe that hell is a real place of conscious, eternal punishment, since the Bible seems so clearly to teach it. For literalists, the Bible is the basis for harmonizing the concept of God's righteousness and justice with His love and mercy. Sensitive literalists believe in a literal, conscious, everlasting hell not because they want to but because the Bible, from their understanding, teaches it.

They believe in a God of justice and righteousness balanced by love and mercy because the Bible teaches it. And if all this exceeds their understanding, they suspend judgment of God's character, believing that they either do not have enough information or enough capacity to understand the subject as God does. They believe that when they stand before Him, and know even as they are known (1 Corinthians 13:12), then it will all be clear. This has been the majority interpretation of the Christian church for two thousand years.

What Is the Metaphorical Interpretation of Hell?

Metaphoricalists believe that hell is a place of endless, conscious, emotional, and spiritual suffering for those who have rejected God in their earthly life.

A metaphor is the use of a word picture to indicate something literal by comparison to it. The "evening of one's life" uses the picture of the closing of day for the approaching end of one's life. As a metaphor, fire, brimstone, and physical torment could be a picture of the reality in hell that is emotional and spiritual torment.

Those who hold to the metaphorical interpretation believe

that hell is eternal torment but not physical torment. They do not believe there is a literal fire. The fire stands for the torment that is a natural consequence of having rejected God and being separated from Him forever.

Speaking about literal physical torture in hell, William Crockett writes:

For some, hellfire is a consequence of having been eternally separated from God.

In Jesus we find someone who genuinely cares for others, who is touched by the sorrows of the people he meets. He never turns his back on the sick and lowly and always counsels kindness in the face of adversity. Yet his words also reveal a grim fate for the wicked. A large sector of people, he says, will be plunged into hell's unquenchable fires (Matthew 7:13–14; 13:42). Could such teaching be true, *literally* true? Will a portion of creation find ease in heaven, while the rest burn in fire?

Faced with such teaching, it is not hard to see why Christians shrink from discussing the doctrine of hell. . . . Jesus believed in hell, but somehow the picture of desperate faces shrieking in a lake of fire unsettles us.

Christians should never be faced with this kind of embarrassment—the Bible does not support a literal view of a burning abyss. Hellfire and brimstone are not literal depictions of hell's furnishings, but figurative expressions warning the wicked of impending doom.

Far from my own theory, I would guess that most evangelicals interpret hell's fires metaphorically, or at least allow for the possibility that hell might be something other than literal fire. "Do not try to imagine what it is like to be in hell," cautions theologian J.I. Packer, ". . . the mistake is to take such pictures as physical descriptions, when in fact they are imagery symbolizing realities . . . far worse than the symbols themselves." Kenneth Kantzer, a former editor of *Christianity Today*, sums up the view of many evangelicals: "The Bible makes it clear that hell is real and it's bad. But when Jesus spoke of flames . . . these are most likely figurative warnings." Likewise, Billy Graham holds a metaphorical view. He comments on the image of fire: "I have often wondered if hell is a terrible burning within our hearts for God, to fellowship with God, a fire that we can never quench" (*Four Views of Hell* 44–45).

One might ask why people believe that the Bible's description of suffering in hell is to be understood metaphorically. The answer is that some Biblical passages are clearly intended to be metaphorical and others are clearly not (see Chapter 3). However, some passages appear to have a little of both interpretations. They are on a kind of middle ground. Whether one holds to literal physical suffering or to spiritual and emotional suffering in hell depends on the interpretation of that middle category of verses that might not be completely clear to some.

For example, the metaphorical view finds it significant that heaven is described in terms familiar with first-century culture. Until the time of gunpowder, all major cities were protected by high, thick walls and sturdy gates, with signs often placed above the gates. Therefore, in Revelation, when heaven is described, it is described in terms relevant to their culture: unimaginably high walls, unbelievably thick. Of course, there is no need for walls in heaven, but that is the way it is pictured anyway. The implication is that heaven is a safe place.

Heaven is also described as a beautiful place. On the walls are twelve kinds of precious stones; yet the stone most precious to us today, the diamond, is not included. Possibly, diamonds were overlooked because, while they were known, they were too difficult to cut and polish, so they were little used and valued. Pearls, on the other hand, were numbered among the most important valuables in the Roman world. Perhaps this is why the massive gates of this city are made from a single pearl.

Hell, like heaven, is sometimes interpreted symbolically.

Heaven is also described as a place of bounty and rest, which would appeal dramatically to a culture in which many people were bound to poverty and labor. People worked from dawn until dusk and ate bread and vegetables. No wonder that they would marvel at sumptuous feasts (Revelation 10:6–9). Clearly, the new heaven and the new earth will be far above and beyond this one in every way. Heaven is beyond our wildest dreams, and to describe it we must think of the most beautiful and wonderful things on earth now and multiply them a hundredfold, and still we will not be grasping its beauty. This is one of the main purposes for metaphor.

The metaphoricalist reasons that if heaven is described in powerful images not intended to be literal but symbolic, so too with hell. The images of hell are the ones that would be the most dramatic and shocking to first-century people, but not to be taken literally. The truth behind the horrible imagery is that hell is a place of profound misery where the unsaved are separated from the presence of God forever, and where they will suffer whatever is the opposite of God and heaven for eternity.

Hell is described as both a place of total darkness as well as a place of fire (Matthew 8:12; 22:13; 25:30; 2 Peter 2:17; Jude 14). But if there is fire, there can be no total darkness. And if there is total darkness, there can be no fire. The writers of these passages, however, were not concerned with seeming conflicts. They described punishment in many ways because they had no clear understanding as to what form it will take. They talked of hell as a place where bodies of the unsaved burned eternally, even though at the same time the bodies are said to be rotting with worms and maggots. At the same time, the bodies receive blows (Luke 12:47). Who inflicts the blows, if they are literal beatings?

For these and other reasons, the metaphorical interpretation does not picture hell as a belching inferno with humans eaten with worms, writhing in agony in a fire that gives no light while someone is beating them. Rather, the unsaved will be cast from the presence of God forever, without any hope of restoration.

C.S. Lewis has written that, since there appear to be degrees of punishment in hell, there might even be relative pleasures for the condemned. Even so, hell would rank as the worst possible place:

> Even if it were possible that the experience . . . of the lost contained no pain and much pleasure, still, that black pleasure would be such as to send any soul, not already damned, flying to its prayers in nightmare terror (*The Problem of Pain* 126).

Lewis is talking about what is often called the pain of missing heaven. This kind of suffering comes not from direct punishment from God—like flames frying the skin eternally—but from having no contact with the One who is the source of love, joy, and peace. Therefore, in such a place, no one can ever know love, joy, or peace, and that is hell. All hope, joy, meaning, and purpose are lost forever, and the resulting emotional and spiritual travail would be easy to understand.

What Is the Conditional View on Hell?

Conditionalists believe that hell is a place of conscious suffering for those who have rejected God in their earthly life, but which eventually ends.

Conditionalists (also known as annihilationists) coincide with a metaphorical view of hell, agreeing that the literal view presents such ghastly specters so out of synch with the character of God and with acceptable methods of interpreting difficult passages. They reject the literal view of hell in favor of a softer condemnation. However, the conditionalist believes that the metaphorical view is little better than the literal view, because human beings are still tortured beyond reason forever. If it is true, as many metaphoricalists suggest, that the suffering is as great, or greater, in the metaphorical view as it is in the literal view, then the metaphorical view is no better than the literalist view. What does it matter if a person writhes in agony from physical anguish or mental anguish. He still writhes in agony, and this seems inconsistent with the character of God to the conditionalist.

Hell has been understood as mental anguish apart from physical torment.

Clark Pinnock, perhaps the most able and enthusiastic proponent of this view has written:

Of all the articles of theology that have troubled the human conscience over the centuries, I suppose few have caused any greater anxiety than the received interpretation of hell as everlasting conscious punishment in body and soul. . . . [W]e are asked to believe that God endlessly tortures sinners by the million, sinners who perish because the Father has decided not to elect them to salvation, though he could have done so.

Not surprisingly, the traditional view of the nature of hell has been a stumbling block for believers and an effective weapon in the hands of skeptics for use against the faith. The situation has become so serious that one scarcely hears hell mentioned at all today, even from pulpits committed to the traditional view. This fact demonstrates that its defenders are not enthusiastic about it, even though the doctrine remains on the books (*Four Views of Hell* 135–6).

The conditionalist view has a number of objections to the literalist view, which, by implication are extended to the metaphorical view.

First, Old Testament words describing the destiny of those who reject God overwhelmingly point to a final, irreversible termination of existence in hell, not to eternal conscious punishment. In Psalm 37, for example, we read that the wicked will fade like grass and wither like the herb, that they will be cut off and be no more, that they will perish and vanish like smoke, and that they will be altogether destroyed. Malachi 4:1 echoes the same imagery:

"Surely the day is coming; it will burn like a furnace. All the arrogant and every evildoer will be stubble, and that day that is coming will set them on fire," says the Lord Almighty. "Not a root or a branch will be left to them."

Second, the Gospels continue this imagery of final destruction. When He warned about God's ability to destroy body and soul in hell, Jesus spoke of judgment in terms that could be understood as final destruction (Matthew 10:28). John the Baptist pictured individuals as dry wood ready to be thrown into the fire, and as chaff about to be burned up (Matthew 3:10, 12). Elsewhere, the wicked were to be burned up just like weeds thrown into the fire (Matthew 13:30, 42, 49–50).

The use of terms like "destroyed" and "burned up" give the impression that the unbeliever can expect to be destroyed by the wrath of God. But when Jesus speaks of the fire not being quenched and the worm dying not, He does not mean that a person is burned forever and eaten by worms forever. He means that the fire is always there and that the worms are always there; they never go away. They are eternal. In other words, no one can ever hope that they will miss out on hell because the fire and the worms died out.

Third, the apostle Paul continued this imagery when he said that everlasting destruction would come upon unrepentant sinners (2 Thessalonians 1:9), and that God would destroy the wicked (1 Corinthians 3:17; Philippians 1:28). "Their destiny is destruction," he stated plainly in Philippians 3:19 (NIV).

Fourth, the apostle Peter spoke of the "destruction of ungodly men" (2 Peter 3:7) and of false teachers who brought upon themselves "swift destruction" (2:1, 3). He said that they would be like the cities of Sodom and Gomorrah, which were burned to ashes, destroyed (2:6). He said that they would perish like the ancient world perished in the great flood (3:6–7). Jude also pointed to Sodom as an analogy to God's final judgment, being the city that underwent "the punishment of eternal fire" (verse 7). The city of Sodom did not burn forever; it burned and was consumed. That is, it was burned once and so forever destroyed. By analogy, a person in the punishment of eternal fire is not burned forever, but, having been burned up, is forever destroyed. It is the fire (probably not literal but symbolic of the wrath of God) that is eternal and the irreversible consequences that are eternal, not the punishment.

Pinnock writes:

A fair person would have to conclude from such texts that the Bible can reasonably be read to teach the final destruction of the wicked. Clearly it has plausibility as an interpretation and integrity as an opinion. It is a natural interpretation of the basic nature of divine judgment. I sincerely hope that traditionalists will stop saying that there is no biblical basis for this view when there is such a strong basis for it.

To the Conditionalist, there is also a strong moral objection to the doctrine of eternal conscious punishment. According to Christian teaching, the nature of God is merciful. God loves the whole world, and he invites sinners to repent and be forgiven of their sins. What would the goodness of God mean if God torments people everlastingly? Of course, the responsible Conditionalist does not criticize God. But the traditional view of the nature of hell does not match well with the character of God as revealed in the Gospels.

Some people have a moral objection to the doctrine of eternal conscious punishment.

People intuitively sense this. There is a powerful moral revulsion against the literal understanding of hell. It pictures God as a bloodthirsty monster who maintains an everlasting Auschwitz for his enemies whom he does not even allow to die. Surely the idea of everlasting conscious torment raises the problem of evil to impossible heights. Anthony Flew was right to object that if Christians really believe that God created people with the full intention of torturing some of them in hell forever, they might as well give up the effort to defend Christianity. John Stott seems to agree: "I find the concept intolerable and do not understand how people can live with it without either cauterizing their feelings or cracking under the strain" (Pinnock 149).

To the conditionalist, the concept of eternal conscious punishment seems neither moral, just, nor required by an exegesis of the biblical texts dealing with hell.

In *Four Views of Hell*, Pinnock strongly affirms the inspiration of Scripture and strongly objects to those who suggest he has gotten soft on Scripture. He believes that the differences he has with traditionalists are a matter of interpretation of the inspired text and not about the issue of the inspiration of that text.

Therefore, he believes in hell, and he believes that some people will go to hell and suffer terrorizing torment in divine judgment for their sin. His only objection to a traditional view of hell is that the torment is eternal.

Of course, the literalists and metaphoricalists point to a passage such as Revelation 14:10–11, which Pinnock concedes is probably the most powerful statement in Scripture to support the traditional viewpoint:

> If anyone worships the beast and his image, and receives his mark on his forehead or on his hand, he himself shall also drink of the wine of the wrath of God. . . . And he shall be tormented with fire and brimstone. . . . And the smoke of their torment ascends forever and ever; and they have no rest day or night.

To this, Pinnock responds:

> While the smoke goes up forever, the text does not say the wicked are tormented forever. It says that they have no relief from their suffering as long as the suffering lasts, but it does not say how long it lasts. As such it could fit hell as annihilation or the traditional view. Before oblivion, there may be a period of suffering, but not unendingly. Besides not teaching the traditional view, the text does not describe the end of history either, which is termed the second death, an image very much in agreement with annihilation (Revelation 20:14) (157).

Conclusion

So here we have a bit of a dilemma, according to the proponents of the three views. None is willing to admit a knockout punch from the others. Many passages about final punishment seem to suggest destruction, whether literal or metaphorical; and Revelation 14 (along with Revelation 20:10) seems to suggest eternal, conscious suffering. Which viewpoint best explains all of Scripture? How can we resolve the seeming contradiction?

Of course, biblical interpreters face similar difficulties with issues such as the relation between the free will of man and the sovereignty of God or the differences between Dispensationalist and Reformed doctrine or between premillennialism and amillennialism. While hell is a serious issue about which people enthusiastically champion strong beliefs, it ought not be allowed to create enmity between people who otherwise believe in the inspiration of Scripture, the perfect character of God, the deity of Christ and the Holy Spirit, the Resurrection, the depravity of humanity, salvation by grace through faith in Jesus, the Great Commission, and the second coming of Christ.

Of course, the one thing that proponents of all three positions agree on is that the Bible teaches that hell is a real place, an unspeakably terrible place of pain, punishment, and destruction. They all agree that Jesus believed in hell and warned people not to go there and that those who do not accept Jesus *will* go there. They all agree that the threat of hell ought to motivate us to share the message of the gospel with others, that we might be used of God to keep people from that dreadful fate.

Speed Bump!

Slow down to be sure you've gotten the main points of this chapter.

Question Answer

Q1. What is the consensus view on hell?

A1. Hell is eternal *separation* from God and all that is good.

Q2. What is the literal view on hell?

A2. Literalists believe that hell is a place of endless, conscious, *physical*, spiritual, and emotional suffering in literal fire for those who have rejected God in their earthly life.

Q3. What is the metaphorical view on hell?

A3. Metaphoricalists believe that hell is a place of endless, conscious, emotional, and *spiritual* suffering for those who have rejected God in their earthly life.

Q4. What is the conditional view on hell?

A4. Conditionalists believe that hell is a place of conscious suffering for those who have rejected God in their earthly life, but which eventually *ends*.

Fill in the Blank

Question Answer

Q1. What is the consensus view on hell?

A1. Hell is eternal _____ from God and all that is good.

Q2. What is the literal view on hell?

A2. Literalists believe that hell is a place of endless, conscious, _____ , spiritual, and emotional suffering in literal fire for those who have rejected God in their earthly life.

Q3. What is the metaphorical view on hell?

A3. Metaphoricalists believe that hell is a place of endless, conscious, emotional, and _____ suffering for those who have rejected God in their earthly life.

Q4. What is the conditional view on hell?

A4. Conditionalists believe that hell is a place of conscious suffering for those who have rejected God in their earthly life, but which eventually _____ .

For Further Thought and Discussion

1. What is the most foreboding aspect of hell in your mind?

2. What role did hell have in your becoming a Christian?

3. Why do you think people don't talk much about hell anymore? What do you think Christians (including pastors and Bible teachers) should do about it?

What If I Don't Believe?

If I don't believe in hell, I ignore one of the clearest teachings in all the Bible, and I erase a compelling reason to be a Christian and to warn others of the danger of not becoming a Christian.

For Further Study

1. Scripture
Several passages in the Bible are central to understanding the subject of hell. They include:

- 2 Kings 23:10

- Matthew 10:28

- Relevation 14:10–11

- Revelation 20:10

2. Books
In studying this subject further I found these volumes very helpful:

Four Views on Hell, William Crockett, ed.
Heaven and Hell, Peter Toon

*Heaven goes by favor. If it went by merit, you would
stay out and your dog would go in.*
■ **Mark Twain**

What Is Heaven?

If you have ever really suffered . . . if you have ever known
heartache, or loneliness, or pain . . . if you have ever been crushed
with remorse over sins committed and longed never to sin again . . .
if you have ever come to realize that this world will never satisfy the
deepest longings of your heart . . . then "heaven" ought to be one of
the most wonderful words in the human vocabulary.

Heaven. The home of the heart's deepest longings. The end of all
suffering, all sorrow, all mourning, all pain. The end of sin.

But it is more than that. Heaven is the beginning of unlimited,
unending joy. It is the presence of righteousness and goodness and
peace. Heaven is the presence of the triune God. It is the beginning of
a life too wonderful even to be imagined in this world.

To those for whom life is easy, to those who are too young, or
have not suffered much, or who are still pinning their hopes for complete happiness on this life, to those who are comfortable in this
world, heaven probably seems distant, irrelevant, possibly even foreboding.

That is the way it seemed to me for so many years. Youth rarely
looks forward to heaven. It is too far away, and youth has its hopes
attached to something more immediate. But as we grow older, as we
realize that the best this world has to offer is not enough, when we finally give up on this world as that which will ever be put right, then
heaven becomes the great hope indeed, the single focus, the Great Expectation that keeps us stable, steadfast, and faithful in this life, while
taking joy from the next.

If there is a hell, there must also be a heaven. If hell is so terrible,
then heaven must be so wonderful. If hell is everlasting destruction,
then heaven is everlasting life.

In this chapter we learn that . . .

1. Heaven is a place of unimaginable beauty and joy.
2. We will worship God, reign with Jesus, and fellowship with one another.
3. We will be sinless images of the triune God.

Vance Havner, a venerable old preacher of a previous generation, once said, "I'm homesick for heaven. It's the hope of heaven that has kept me alive this long." Another time, he said, "There are a lot of questions the Bible doesn't answer about the Hereafter. But I think one reason is illustrated by the story of a boy sitting down to a bowl of spinach when there's a chocolate cake at the end of the table. He's going to have a rough time eating that spinach when his eyes are on the cake. And if the Lord had explained everything to us about what's ours to come, I think we'd have a rough time with our spinach down here."

And so it is. The Bible says that there is a heaven, and it gives some indication of what it is, but it doesn't come close to satisfying our curiosity. However, we can be enriched by discovering what the Bible does tell us about that great place. To answer the questions we have about heaven, we can look at specific Scripture passages and do a little educated speculating as well.

What Is Heaven Like?

Heaven is a place of unimaginable beauty and joy.

From the biblical language, is seems that heaven is a real place, not a state of mind or peaceful condition, or a retirement village for disembodied spirits. When Jesus revealed Himself to His disciples after His resurrection, he appeared in a real body capable of talking, walking, and eating (John 21:1–23). And the apostle Paul taught that our bodies will be like Jesus' (Philippians 3:21). This indicates that we will live physical lives rather than haunt shadowy corners of the universe.

Why I need to know this

I need to know this so that I will look forward to heaven, so that I can gain emotional strength for the trials of today by looking forward to the joys of heaven.

This is strengthened by the understanding that God created heaven (Genesis 1:1) and that Jesus went there after He was resurrected (John 14:1–3). When Jesus ascended into heaven, the whole point seems to be that He went to a specific place. In Acts 1:9, we read:

> Now when He had spoken these things, while they watched, He was taken up, and a cloud received Him out of their sight. And while they looked steadfastly toward heaven as He went up, behold, two men stood by them in white apparel, who also said, "Men of Galilee, why do you stand gazing up into heaven? This same Jesus, who was taken up from you into heaven, will so come in like manner as you saw Him go into heaven."

The biblical story of Stephen, the first Christian martyr, leaves a similar impression. While he was being stoned and just before he died, Stephen, "full of the Holy Spirit, gazed into heaven and saw the glory of God, and Jesus standing at the right hand of God, and said, 'Look! I see the heavens opened and the Son of Man standing at the right hand of God!' " (Acts 7:54–60). And Paul says that he was caught up to the "third heaven" (2 Corinthians 12:1–10).

There are commonly thought to be three uses of the word heaven: the atmosphere around the earth, the starry heavens of the universe, and the place where God dwells (which is often understood as the third heaven). If the first two are "places" it seems likely that the third is also a place, where physical beings like the resurrected Jesus can live. Since we will have resurrection bodies like Jesus', it seems reasonable to conclude that there is a physical place where these rather physical bodies can function.

Further, our heavenly existence includes a renewed earth that will be part of our celestial existence, along with a celestial city, the New Jerusalem (Revelation 21). One of the most striking features about the renewed earth is that it will have no oceans (Revelation 21:1). Beyond that, we can only speculate, drawing on the descriptions of the original creation in Genesis

Our heavenly life will be a paradise that is currently beyond our comprehension.

1–2. Clearly, what little we know about it now still makes it a grand paradise, even if it is beyond our comprehension.

Beyond the renewed earth, we see a heavenly city in which

the throne of God and Jesus rests, suggesting that it is the place into which Jesus ascended (Ephesians 2:6) and the place into which Stephen looked as he was being stoned.

In Revelation 21–22, we read that it is a "holy city," and that "there shall by no means enter it anything that defiles, or causes an abomination or a lie." It is a place prepared as a bride adorned for her husband (21:2). If you have ever been on the "inside" of a wedding, this phrase means a great deal to you. Brides spend months, usually, preparing for their wedding day. Everything must be just so. The dress must be made or ordered and fitted. The right veil must be chosen. Attendants must be recruited to escort the bride during the ceremony. The church must be decorated. There's a rehearsal; then the ceremony.

Before the bride is seen, the groom and his groomsmen come in with the minister. Then a flower girl and ring-bearer walk down the aisle, followed by a succession of attendants. Then the music changes, intensifying and increasing in volume. It is a signal. Everyone in the sanctuary rises. Then, and only then, when all the life-consuming preparations have been made, the bride makes her entrance. Short of our entrance into heaven, few of us have so much focused attention as the moment a bride steps into view in a church wedding. Using this imagery, the apostle John describes the New Jerusalem as having been prepared as a bride adorned for her husband. It's hard to imagine what an omniscient and omnipotent God could create in two thousand years that would live up to such a buildup!

It is a place where "God will wipe away every tear . . ." and "there shall be no more death, nor sorrow, nor dying; and there shall be no more pain" (21:4). There we will drink from the fountain of the water of life freely (21:6). It is a city that has the "glory of God" and its radiance is like a rare jewel (21:11).

If the dimensions in Revelation are to be taken literally, it is a city of immense size, being nearly 1500 miles long, wide, and high (21:16). To get some feel for this, when you see pictures of astronauts orbiting the earth, with the earth *waaaaay* down there, the astronauts are only approximately 200 miles above the earth. The New Jerusalem would be seven times taller than that. In addition to its outer size, there are twelve stories inside this giant cube, so each story would have a ceiling approximately one hundred miles above the "streets of gold." No one will feel cramped in there. The city has walls constructed of immense precious jewels (21:18–21), with gates of single, immense pearls (21:21). Surely it will be more beautiful and immense than Yosemite Valley or the Swiss Alps or the Grand Canyon. If we marvel at those stupendous sights, what will we do when we see heaven?

Whether or not the description of the city is intended to be literal or symbolic, we have no trouble concluding that the size of heaven is immense, and its beauty overwhelming.

The writer of Hebrews says that we do not yet see everything in subjection to man (Hebrews 2:8). This suggests that some day all things will be subject to us as we reign with Christ. This will fulfill God's original design in creation and, in that sense, redeemed humanity will "inherit the earth" (Matthew 5:5) and rule over it as God originally intended.

It should come as no surprise, then, that many of the things we will do in heaven are very physical things, like eating and drinking at the marriage supper of the Lamb (Revelation 19:9). In heaven, Jesus will once again share the cup with His disciples **We will do some very physical things in heaven.** (Luke 22:18). A river, of the water of life, will flow through the middle of the streets of heaven (Revelation 22:1). The tree of life will bear twelve kinds of fruit (Revelation 22:2). While some believe these are symbolic representations of fellowship and life, many Bible teachers understand them as literal, even while they suggest larger spiritual truths.

What Will We Do in Heaven?

We will worship God, reign with Jesus, and fellowship with one another.

Beyond the heartening and stupefying size and beauty of heaven, it is more important to understand that in heaven we will enjoy eternal fellowship with God the Father, Jesus, and the Holy Spirit (three, yet one). Also, we will reign over the universe as vice-regents of Jesus, and we will have eternal fellowship with the rest of God's people from all nations and all periods of history.

Worship God. I know what it's like to be bored in church. As a four- or five-year-old child, I remember being scolded by my grandmother because I had found an empty pew all to myself, where I had lain down and then crawled, twisted, squirmed, and banged my shoes against the mahogany pews. Instead of "be-having" and paying attention in church, I made a general dis-traction of myself. I have never done that again, on the outside, but on the inside, I have done it many times. The most recent time was not long ago!

I have sat through over forty years of church services, in-cluding services at a Christian college where I went to church twice on Sunday, once in the middle of the week, and to daily chapel services. I did the same thing for four years during semi-nary. I did the same thing when I taught in a Christian college for several years. I have been bored so many times in church that I would be a wealthy man if I had been paid an hourly wage for every hour I have been bored in church.

So I realize that it will not make heaven sound too appealing to some of us to say that the first thing we will do there is wor-ship God. This often conjures up a picture of people sitting on clouds picking listlessly at harp strings, bored to tears after a million years, trying to think of a new tune.

On the other hand, have you ever been in a terrific worship service, where everything was special and meaningful, for you and others? Sometimes it was like that in seminary for me when hundreds of voices would sing some of the great hymns of the faith: powerful and melodic voices heralding eternal truth with strong conviction and deep emotion. It was always deeply mov-ing. Our seminary hymn was *All Hail the Power of Jesus' Name*. I believe nearly everyone who ever graduated from my *alma mater* knows all the stanzas by heart and loves that song with an inor-dinate love because it is linked with so many wonderful memo-ries.

When I hear that hymn today, it is hard for me to sing be-cause a peach pit slowly forms in my throat, hot tears well up in my eyes, and my lower lip quivers spastically. Oh, what a grand and moving experience! It is one of life's great joys to be back at seminary and stand alongside thousands of others who feel like I do about that song. I worship deeply. I am filled with gratitude to God. I am certainly not bored.

I have been in conferences where thousands of people have sung well-known hymns with the same gusto, and it is deeply moving. I am not bored. The more people present, the more deeply they believe what they are singing, the more moving it is.

Now, transfer your thoughts to heaven. There are millions

upon millions of voices. Each one is more beautiful than any voice on earth has ever been. The triune God is there. You are surrounded with beauty that makes Yosemite Valley look like a wall mural. All the people sing with deeper conviction and meaning than you have ever heard on earth.

Even the best worship on earth will pale by comparison to any worship in heaven.

We glimpse this in Revelation 5, where we see God on His throne and an emerald rainbow around the throne. Lightning and thunder flash and boom in the background. Dignitaries dressed in beautiful white robes and gold crowns sit around the throne. Angels hover in the air. Jesus is there. Many angels (ten thousand times ten thousand) sing with deafening grandeur:

> *Worthy is the Lamb who was slain*
> *To receive power and riches and wisdom,*
> *And strength and honor and glory and blessing!* (v. 12)
> *Blessing and honor and glory and power*
> *Be to Him who sits on the throne,*
> *And to the Lamb, forever and ever!* (v. 13).

Have you ever been to a grand performance of the *Messiah*, one with a two-hundred-voice choir and a fifty-piece orchestra? When you hear the angels singing in heaven, that performance of *Messiah* will sound like Alvin and the Chipmunks by comparison.

You will not be bored.

In addition to worshiping, we will also have fellowship with God. The apostle John wrote, "Beloved, now we are children of God; and it has not yet been revealed what we shall be, but we know that when He is revealed, we shall be like Him, for we shall see Him as He is" (1 John 3:2). Imagine. We will see God face to face. And if Jesus' experience with His disciples is any indication, we will have fellowship with Jesus too. After His resurrection, Jesus made it a point to come back and visit His disciples (John 21). And He said in Revelation 3:20, "Behold, I stand at the door and knock. If anyone hears My voice and opens the door, I will come in to him and dine with him, and he with Me." If Jesus desires fellowship with us before we are resurrected, how much more after we are resurrected?

Who is the one person in the world you would most like to

meet? A famous musician, a statesman, a king, a queen? The girl
or boy next door? If you could meet that person, after longing for
it so earnestly, your life would be complete for that moment. You
would be satisfied for that one hour or day that you got to talk to
Billy Graham or Mother Teresa or Itzhak Perlman or Queen Eliz-
abeth or the President or the person next door. Perhaps you
would like to meet a historical figure, such as the apostle Paul or
George Washington or Winston Churchill. If you met that person, you would not be looking out the window or glancing at
your watch. You would be, for that moment, complete, satisfied,
totally occupied with that person. So it will be when we meet Jesus. We will be complete and satisfied in His presence, and it will
not be temporary but forever.

Reign with Jesus. If you can't get your kids to clean up their
bedrooms, if you get nervous, if there are more than three people
present when you speak, if you have trouble just getting to work
on time, then you can't imagine reigning with Christ in heaven.
But it will happen. When you get your new body, it will come
with capacities never imagined on earth. Same with your mind.
[Christ] "will transform the body of our humble state into con-
formity with the body of His glory, by the exertion of the power
that He has even to subject all things to Himself" (Philippians
3:21).

We don't know what it means to reign with Christ, but we
have some hints. One is 1 Corinthians 6. Paul is chastening believers for suing each other in secular courts. "Dare any of you,
having a matter against another, go to law before the unrighteous, and not before the saints?" Then, he asks two extravagant
questions with the calmness of someone asking to pass the
mashed potatoes. "Do you not know that the saints will judge
the world?" (verse 2), and, "Do you not know that we shall
judge angels?" (verse 3).

So! We will judge the world and angels, will we? Even my
aunt Bea, who is always humble, friendly, forever smiling, and
almost totally non-assertive? Even my aunt Bea, who makes
mouth-watering pies and cakes and homemade noodles? Even
my aunt Bea, who devoted her life to her church, her husband,
her children, her kitchen, her garden? Is she also going to judge
the world and angels? Apparently. But how? It will be with a
new body and a new mind that will be perfectly capable of it.
She'll do a fine job of it. She may well rule over saints who were

politicians or presidents of large companies, but who were careless about their devotion to Christ.

In addition, Romans 8:16–17 says, "The Spirit Himself bears witness with our spirit that we are children of God, and if children, then heirs—heirs of God and joint heirs with Christ, if indeed we suffer with Him, that we may also be glorified together." Yes, what Christ inherits we inherit. As He was raised up into heavenly places, so we are raised up into heavenly places, to be seated with Him (Ephesians 2:6–7). In Revelation 20:6, we read that we shall be "priests of God and of Christ, and shall reign with Him."

But what does it mean exactly? What are the specifics? Who knows? In her book *Heaven . . . Your Real Home,* Joni Erickson Tada speculates:

Reigning with Christ brings an inexhaustible potential to us.

> Maybe our reign on earth will include lifting up the poor and the needy of Kurdistan, reforesting the hills of Lebanon, helping to judge the wicked, or planting trees along the Amazon. How about clearing the slums of Rio de Janeiro or getting rid of nuclear waste? Maybe we'll teach the nations how to worship God, as well as a new definition of peace and how to beat their swords into plowshares. Shall we do a patch job on the ozone layer and make the Blue Danube absolutely azure rather than mud-brown? Cut government fat, get rid of red tape, and show everyone that a theocracy is the only rule in town?
>
> One thing's for sure. There will be no shelters for the homeless (no homeless men and women!). No orphanages or mental hospitals. No abortion clinics. And no nursing homes for old people (69).

When the Lord creates the new heaven and new earth, many of these possibilities may be automatically eliminated, but I thought her speculation was interesting. It painted hypothetical possibilities that, while maybe not likely, showed the practicality and worth of many things we may be doing in reigning with Christ.

Perhaps new worlds will be created in other galaxies, and like Adam and Eve we will be capable of beginning at a beginning, and creating something from scratch, to the glory of God a million years later. Then, perhaps we'll get together to see how my world differs from yours, but how they are both beautiful and bring glory to God.

Fellowship with One Another. Christ created a body on earth, spiritual stones, which together make up a "dwelling place of God in the Spirit." The church is the body of Christ, and one of its prime goals is to express the unity that exists for it potentially. This is possible because all of its "members" are connected to one another to form the whole. Here on earth, stuck in imperfection, we do not experience that full unity. Bible teacher J. Vernon McGee used to say, "To live above with saints we love, oh, that will be glory. To live below with saints we know, well, that's another story." And so it is. Fellowship down here is imperfect and often broken. But up there, not so. It will be perfect and whole.

The apostle Paul urged us here on earth to "keep the unity of the Spirit in the bond of peace" (Ephesians 4:3). In heaven, we will have unimpeded unity and fellowship with all the other members of the body of Christ.

Have you ever been in a quiet, intimate conversation and felt you were experiencing something special? Do you have special friends with whom intimate conversation is natural? Have you ever been among people rooting for an athletic team, or filling sandbags during a flood, or helping a family whose home had burned down? That sense of bonding with the people will be with us in heaven, I believe. And much, much more.

In *Immortality*, Habermas and Morgan write:

> [T]he collective aspect of heavenly activity promises to be a blessed one. Old Testament theology emphasized the resurrection of the entire nation—the righteous would rise together (Isaiah 26:19; Daniel 12:1–3). In the New Testament, Paul speaks of the resurrection of the dead in the plural: Dead and living believers will be raised together, sharing in this marvelous event (1 Thessalonians 4:16–17). So we will be reunited with our believing loved ones who died before us. Many other passages indicate the fellowship believers will share with each other in heaven (Matthew 8:11; 1 Corinthians 12:13; Revelation 21:26–27). Even our praise to God in heaven will be done together (Revelation 5:11–13) (145–146).

In heaven, it will be all for one and one for all!

There will be great feasts (Matthew 8:11), a wonderful wedding ceremony (Revelation 19:7–9), glorious worship experiences (Revelation 5:15; 19:1–8). It will be all for one and one for all!

What Will We Be Like in Heaven?
We will be sinless images of the triune God.

The Bible teaches that humanity was created in the image of God. That image was marred, however, by sin. Humanity was lost, and God planned its salvation; He would send His Son to die for humanity's sins. Those who receive God's offer of salvation are restored to life with God, and the image of God within them is restored.

In heaven, we will reflect the image of God in a way we could never do in this life. Sin will be done away with, and we will be free to become all that the will of God allows us to become. What all that includes is not yet known, but I will never forget reading C.S. Lewis's observation that if we were to see our glorified selves walking down the street, we would be tempted to fall at our feet and worship ourselves. I suspect he is right.

If our bodies are like Jesus' body, as we noted earlier, we will be able to appear and disappear at will, to pass through walls or doors without limitation, to rise from the ground unbound by gravity, and apparently to travel at the speed of thought, since any other speed would be much too slow. It would take 100,000 light-years just to get from one side of our galaxy to the other, and there are 100 billion known galaxies.

In the ages to come, we will continue to grow and "become" forever.

But beyond our physical abilities, the spiritual abilities will be the most special. Of course, those who have physical pain or limitations will be more appreciative of perfect bodies than others, but even after they have received new bodies, their spirits will continue to grow and become and be fulfilled.

Ephesians 2:7 states that "in the ages to come He might show the exceeding riches of His grace in His kindness toward us in Christ Jesus." We will continue to grow and "become" forever. Even though we will have resurrected bodies, we will still be finite beings, held in awe of an infinite God. We will still "wonder" and "marvel." Our mouths will still drop open, goose bumps will still play up and down our spine, amazement will still fill our soul.

Our longings for intimacy, fellowship, peace, safety, and rest will be fulfilled. Ecclesiastes 3:11 says that God has placed eternity in our hearts. We have a longing for eternal existence, to be free from the ticking clock, free from impending death. One of the primary characteristics of the heroes chronicled in Hebrews 11 is that they were strangers on this earth. They were people of whom the world was not worthy, people who longed for a "better, that is a heavenly country. Therefore God is not ashamed to be called their God, for He has prepared a city for them" (verse 16). This better place, this eternal place, will fulfill the deepest longings of the heart. Why? Because God gave us the longings in the first place, and it is He who has planned from eternity past to fulfill them.

Conclusion

What will we be like in heaven? We will be like a thirsty person who has finally had his driving thirst quenched. Like a hungry person who has finally had his fill. Like a lonely person finally reunited with loved ones. Like a person on the gallows receiving news of a pardon.

In Deuteronomy 8:2–3, we read:

Remember how the Lord your God led you all the way in the desert these forty years, to humble you and to test you in order to know what was in your heart, whether or not you would keep his commands. He humbled you, *causing you to hunger and then feeding you with manna* . . . to teach you that man does not live on bread alone but on every word that comes from the mouth of the Lord (NIV, emphasis added).

We will be "those who hungered" and then were fed by God. We hunger for Him and the perfection He gives. Our food is God and His creation and His people.

Speed Bump!
Slow down to be sure you've gotten the main points from this chapter.

Question & Answer

Q1. What is heaven like?

A1. Heaven is a place of unimaginable beauty and *joy*.

Q2. What will we do in heaven?

A2. We will *worship* God, reign with Jesus, and fellowship with one another.

Q3. What will we be like in heaven?

A3. We will be sinless *images* of the triune God.

Fill in the Blanks

Question
Answer

Q1. What is heaven like?

A1. Heaven is a place of unimaginable beauty and _____.

Q2. What will we do in heaven?

A2. We will _____ God, reign with Jesus, and fellowship with one another.

Q3. What will we be like in heaven?

A3. We will be sinless _____ of the triune God.

For Further Thought and Discussion

1. What was your concept of heaven before reading this chapter?

2. How has it changed? What other things about heaven do you believe?

3. What role did heaven play in your decision to become a Christian?

4. What role do you think heaven should play in talking to others about becoming Christian?

What If I Don't Believe?

If I don't believe in heaven, I reject a major teaching of the Bible, and I lose one of the great hopes of life. I lose one of the great motivations and sources of strength for enduring the difficulties of this life, because I have nothing lasting to look forward to. I have no great hope to share with others as to how God will set things right in the future. I cannot see how all the difficulties of this life will be worth it all when I see Jesus.

For Further Study

1. Scripture
There are several key passages that are important in studying this subject further. They include:

- Acts 1:9–11
- John 14:1–3
- Romans 8:16–17
- Revelation 20:6
- 1 Corinthians 6:2–3
- Revelation 4—5
- Revelation 21—22

2. Books
There are several books which are helpful in studying this subject further. They include:

Heaven, Your Real Home, Joni Erickson Tada
Heaven Help Us! Steve Lawson
Eternity, Joseph Stowell

While time lasts there will always be a future, and that future will hold both good and evil since the world is made to that mingled pattern.
■ **Dorothy Sayers**

11

Will All Prophecies Be Fulfilled?

Someone once asked the philosopher Hegel about the meaning of a very abstract and difficult thesis he had written. I don't have the exact quote, but his response was something like, "My friend, when I wrote that, only two people knew the meaning. Myself and God. Now, unfortunately, only one person knows. God!"

That is similar to biblical prophecy. There is much about it that only God knows. We think we know some of it, and we probably do. There are other prophecies we think we know, but when we get to heaven we will discover that we were mistaken. And there are some prophecies whose meanings we realize we don't know for sure, even though we may have opinions. We can be confident, however, that all true prophecies will be fulfilled eventually.

In this chapter we learn that . . .

1. The biblical prophets were not fortune-tellers but spokespersons for God.
2. The prophetic message included foretelling and forthtelling.
3. The accuracy of past fulfilled prophecies plus the character of God give us complete confidence that unfulfilled prophecies will be fulfilled.

How can we have that confidence? There are several reasons, ranging all the way from the qualifications of a prophet in the Old Testament to the character of the God who gave the prophecies. Add to that the amazing record of prophecies already fulfilled, and we can have quite a bit of confidence that all biblical prophecies will be fulfilled.

What Were Prophets in the Bible?

The biblical prophets were not fortune-tellers but spokespersons for God.

Prophets in the Bible did some pretty amazing things. They made ax heads float in water (2 Kings 6:6), they called down fire from heaven (1 Kings 18:38), they struck rocks and water poured out (Exodus 17:6), they foretold the future with absolute accuracy (Deuteronomy 18:20). With such stupendous credits to their names, the primary task of a prophet may be overlooked. The primary meaning of the word "prophet" is "spokesperson." And the main function of a biblical prophet was to be a spokesperson for God.

We see a good example in Exodus where the Lord commissioned Moses to speak to Pharaoh. Moses objected on the grounds that he was not an accomplished speaker:

> So the Lord said to Moses: "See, I have made you as God to Pharaoh, and Aaron your brother shall be your prophet. You shall speak all that I command you. And Aaron your brother shall speak to Pharaoh . . ." (Exodus 7:1–2 NASB).

How clear it is. A prophet speaks for someone else.

Therefore, the prophets in the Bible were people who spoke the Word of God to other people. Often, this word was revealed directly to the prophet by God. At other times the prophet simply taught and exhorted the people regarding things that had been previously revealed and possibly written down.

Why I need to know this

I need to know this so that I can have confidence and trust that the unfulfilled biblical prophecies, such as Jesus' second coming, will actually occur. I can also discount the tabloid newspapers' prophets as false prophets at best.

Men and women of pagan traditions were often magicians, using amazingly advanced tricks to fool people into thinking they had supernatural powers (Exodus 7:11). Other times, people were in league with demons, and demonic powers gave them supernatural ability (Acts 16:16–19), which they exploited to gain spiritual power over others.

The biblical prophet was quite a different figure. His task was to wait for God to speak. He did not force God. Rather, it was God who called the prophet and initiated the message to the prophet, and then the prophet was to transmit the message exactly as he heard it (Jeremiah 20:7). Further, people were obligated to respond as though God, Himself, had spoken:

> I will raise up a prophet from among their countrymen like you, and I will put My words in his mouth, and he shall speak to them all that I command him. And it shall come about that whoever will not listen to My words which he shall speak in My name, I Myself will require it of him (Deuteronomy 18:18–19).

This was the role and force of a prophet of God.

The role of the prophet evolved somewhat, so that by the time of the New Testament a prophet had a broader role, which included messages of encouragement, consolation, and exhortation to more faithful living (1 Corinthians 14:3–4). However, it also included the lofty work of proclaiming words from the risen Christ (John 16:12–14; Revelation 1:10, 4:1–2). Like Old Testament prophecy, this new prophetic message was an immediate communication of God's Word to His people through the prophet (Revelation 16:15; 22:7).

Since the prophet was such an authoritative person in Jewish and Christian life, it is no surprise that those who were not true prophets tried to convince people that they were God's prophets. Jesus and the apostles predicted that

A biblical prophet carried a lot of authority in Jewish and Christian life.

false prophets would arise (Matthew 24:11; 1 John 4:1). We make the point, however, that true prophets were not just people who went around predicting the future. They were spokespersons for God. Whenever God revealed a message to them that included information about the future, they passed it on as faithful messengers. They were not, however, seers, or fortune-tellers. In fact, that practice was forbidden in the Mosaic Law:

> There shall not be found among you anyone who makes his son or his daughter pass through the fire, or one who practices witchcraft, or a soothsayer, or one who interprets omens, or a sorcerer, or one who conjures spells, or a medium, or a spiritist, or one who calls up the dead. For all who do these things are an abomination to the Lord, and because of these abominations the Lord your God drives them out from before you (Deuteronomy 18:10–12).

What Two Kinds of Prophet's Messages Did the Prophets Speak?

The prophetic message included foretelling and forthtelling.

By foretelling, we mean the times the prophet revealed the future. For example, Elijah's prophecy to Ahab, king of Israel, about a long spell of drought that was approaching. In 1 Kings 17:1, we read:

And Elijah the Tishbite, of the inhabitants of Gilead, said to Ahab, "As the Lord God of Israel lives, before whom I now stand, there shall not be dew nor rain these years, except at my word." And sure enough, there wasn't!

Other times, a prophecy referred to an event far into the distant future, such as the coming of the Messiah:

Rejoice greatly, O daughter of Zion! Shout, in triumph O daughter of Jerusalem! Behold, your king is coming to you; He is just and endowed with salvation (Zechariah 9:9 NASB).

This was also true of Christ's return:

But I do not want you to be ignorant, brethren, concerning those who have fallen asleep, lest you sorrow as others who have no hope. For if we believe that Jesus died and rose again, even so, God will bring with Him those who sleep in Jesus. For this we say to you by the word of the Lord, that we who are alive and remain until the coming of the Lord will by no means precede those who are asleep. For the Lord Himself will descend from heaven with a shout, with the voice of an archangel, and with the trumpet of God. And the dead in Christ will rise first. Then we who are alive and remain shall be caught up together with them in the clouds to meet the Lord in the air. And thus we shall always be with the Lord (1 Thessalonians 4:13–17).

Forthtelling is different than foretelling. Forthtelling declares how God's people should live and what will happen to them if they do not live that way. There were typically three elements, overall, to a prophet's forthtelling message: the indictment, the warning, and the appeal, though not every element of the message occurs each time the prophet spoke.

By indictment, we mean that the prophet declared exactly what people were doing wrong. For example, in 2 Samuel, Nathan came to King David after he, David, had committed adultery with the wife of one of his generals and then had that general killed. Using an object lesson, Nathan asked David what should happen to a wealthy man who possessed many sheep but who selfishly stole the pet lamb of a poor man, killed it, and ate it. David exploded! "As the Lord lives, the man who has done this shall surely die!" Nathan said to David, "You are the man!" (12:5, 7). The prophet Nathan indicted David in the name of the Lord. He declared him guilty by the authority of God Himself.

The second element, warning, declares what God would do if those spoken to did not repent. In David's case, the warning was really a pronouncement of judgment, because in that

Biblical prophets indicted, warned, and appealed.

instance God did not allow David to escape all the consequences. Nathan declared that "the sword shall never depart from your house," and "I will take your wives before your eyes and give them to your neighbor, and he shall lie with your wives in the sight of this sun. For you did it secretly, but I will do this thing before all Israel" (verses 11–12).

David repented of his sin, so God forgave him and as a result, Nathan said, "The Lord also has put away your sin; you shall not die. However, because by this deed you have given great occasion to the enemies of the Lord to blaspheme, the child also who is born to you shall surely die" (verses 13–14).

The third element of forthtelling, appeal, declares that if the people stop sinning God will forgive and not judge them. For example, the prophet Jonah warned the people of Nineveh to repent or in forty days it would be overthrown. The city responded, with its king calling for a citywide fast to demonstrate repentance. "Then God saw their works, that they turned from their evil way; and God relented from the disaster that He had said He would bring upon them, and He did not do it" (Jonah 3:10).

We see, then, that the prophetic message sometimes painted a picture of the future (foretelling), and sometimes it warned people of judgment and appealed for repentance (forthtelling).

The ultimate test as to whether a prophet was a true prophet of God was if the prophecies came true. A prophet was required to be 100% accurate, and if he was not he was to be stoned:

> But the prophet who presumes to speak a word in My name, which I have not commanded him to speak, or who speaks in the name of other gods, that prophet shall die. And if you say in your

heart, "How shall we know the word which the Lord has not spoken?"—when a prophet speaks in the name of the Lord, if the thing does not happen or come to pass, that is the thing which the Lord has not spoken; the prophet has spoken it presumptuously; you shall not be afraid of him (Deuteronomy 18:22).

What Confidence Can We Have in Prophecies Not Yet Fulfilled?

The accuracy of past fulfilled prophecies plus the character of God give us complete confidence that unfulfilled prophecies will be fulfilled.

In an earlier volume in this series on the subject of Jesus, I talked about the significance of past fulfilled prophecies, and how the reliability of past fulfilled prophecies gives us confidence that future unfulfilled prophecies, such as the second coming of Christ, will be fulfilled:

The record of fulfilled Old Testament prophecies speaks for itself.

There are many prophecies in the Old Testament which Jesus fulfilled, some of them more obvious than others. For our purposes, we will focus on the more obvious ones. So that you can see them most clearly, I would like to just state the Old Testament prophecy briefly, and then the fulfillment we see in the New Testament. Let the record speak for itself.

1. *Prophecy:* The Messiah would be born of a virgin. "Therefore the Lord Himself will give you a sign: Behold a virgin will be with Child and bear a son, and she will call His name Immanuel (Isaiah 7:14).

   Fulfillment: Jesus was born of the virgin Mary. "She was found to be with child by the Holy Spirit. And Joseph . . . kept her a virgin until she gave birth to a Son; and he called His name Jesus" (Matt. 1:17–25).

2. *Prophecy:* That the Messiah would be born of the ancestry of King David. "Behold the days are coming, declares the Lord, when I shall raise up for David a righteous Branch; and He will reign as King and act wisely and do justice and righteousness in the land (Jeremiah 23:5).

   Fulfillment: In the genealogy in the Gospel of Luke, Jesus is listed as being in the lineage of David. "Jesus . . . the son of David" (Luke 3:23, 31).

3. *Prophecy:* The Messiah would be born in the city of Bethlehem. "But as for you, Bethlehem . . . too little to be among the clans of Judah, from you One will go forth for Me to be ruler in Israel. His goings forth are from long ago, from the days of eternity" (Micah 5:2).

   Fulfillment: Jesus was born in Bethlehem. "For unto you this day in the city of David (Bethlehem) there has been born to you a Savior, who is Christ the Lord" (Luke 2:11).

   These prophecies have to do with the birth of Jesus, the Messiah. There are other remarkable prophecies concerning his death, some of them in the Old Testament, and some of them in the Gospels.

4. *Prophecy:* The Messiah would be betrayed by a friend. "Even my close friend, in whom I trusted, who ate my bread, has lifted up his heel against me" (Psalm 41:9).

   Fulfillment: Jesus was betrayed by Judas Iscariot, one of His twelve disciples. "Judas Iscariot, the one who betrayed Him" (Matthew 10-4).

5. *Prophecy:* The Messiah would be tortured and crucified. "But He was pierced through for our transgressions, He was bruised for our iniquities. The chastening for our well-being fell upon Him, and by His stripes, we are healed" (Isaiah 53:5).

   Fulfillment: Jesus was beaten and then crucified. "Then he (Pilate) released Barabbas for them; but Jesus he scourged and delivered over to be crucified" (Matthew 27:26).

6. *Prophecy:* Jesus would rise from the dead. "For Thou wilt not abandon my soul to Sheol (the place of the departed dead); neither wilt Thou allow Thy Holy One to see decay" (Psalm 16:10).

   Fulfillment: Jesus rose from the dead. "And the angel answered and said to the women, 'Do not be afraid; for I know that you are looking for Jesus who has been crucified. He is not here, for He has risen, just as He said. Come, see the place where He was lying' " (Matt. 28:5-6).

   We could go on and on with many more prophecies and fulfillments. I have just selected a few of the major ones to give an idea of Jesus' remarkable life as it fulfilled one after another of the prophecies that told of the Messiah, in some cases, thousands of years before He was born. Again, in *Evidence that Demands a Verdict* (167), we see that the chance that any man might have lived down to the present time and fulfilled just eight of the major prophecies that Jesus fulfilled are 1 in 10 to the 17th power. That is, one, in 100,000,000,000,000,000. In order to help us comprehend these staggering odds, suppose we take this many silver dollars (10 to the 17th power) and lay them on the face of Texas. Now, as you know, Texas is a big state. If you could flip Texas west using El Paso as a hinge, Houston would land in the Pacific Ocean. If you could flip Texas east, using Houston as a hinge, El Paso would land in the Atlantic. If you could flip Texas north using the top of the panhandle as a hinge, the lowest part of Texas would land just

We have no reason to doubt the fulfillment of God's as yet unfulfilled prophecies.

short of the Canadian border. Texas is a big state. This many silver dollars (10 to the 17th power) would cover the entire state two feet deep in silver dollars. Now imagine that one of those silver dollars was painted red. Blindfold a man and tell him that he can travel anywhere in the state he wants to, and pick up one silver dollar. Keep in mind that traveling at 70 miles per hour, you cannot drive

across Texas in a day. His chances of getting the marked silver dollar are approximately the same as a person fulfilling eight major prophecies of the Messiah by chance. Now, consider that there are 48 prophecies that Jesus fulfilled. The odds that any one man fulfilled all 48 by chance are 10 to the 157th power. There is no practical way to even illustrate that number. Let's just say that there is about as good a chance of a tornado going through a junk yard and assembling a perfect automobile. When we look at the fulfilled prophecies in the life of Christ, the Bible becomes a very convincing book, and Jesus becomes a very convincing Messiah, God the Son. (*What You Need to Know about Jesus* 131–134).

Not only do we have these convincing fulfillments of past prophecy, but we have the character of God to rely on that future prophecies will be fulfilled. In Hebrews 6:18, where we read that "it is impossible for God to lie." If God has said it, it will happen, or there is no reliable God. If God is good, and we believe He is (1 Timothy 4:4; 3 John 11), and if He is all-powerful, and we believe He is (Job 42:4), and all-knowing, and we believe He is (Psalm 139:2–4), then He can be relied on to carry out any plan He conceives ahead of time.

He said He would bring a Savior, and He did. He said the Savior will come again, and we can believe with godly confidence that He will. Time and time again our all-knowing, all-powerful, good and reliable God has proven Himself faithful in the past. Therefore we have no reason to doubt His prophecies about the future.

Conclusion

In conclusion, prophecy in Scripture includes two dimensions: foretelling and forthtelling. Sometimes prophets predicted the future and sometimes they merely proclaimed the Word of God regarding holy living. Because of all the past prophecies that have been fulfilled and because of the character of God, we can have complete assurance that all unfulfilled prophecies will one day be fulfilled.

Speed Bump!

Slow down to be sure you've gotten the main points from this chapter.

Question **A**nswer

Q1. What were prophets in the Bible?

A1. The biblical prophets were not fortune-tellers but *spokespersons* for God.

Q2. What two kinds of messages did the prophet speak?

A2. The prophetic message included *foretelling* and *forthtelling.*

Q3. What confidence can we have in prophecies not yet fulfilled?

A3. The accuracy of *past* fulfilled prophecies plus the character of God give us complete confidence that unfulfilled prophecies will be fulfilled.

Fill in the Blank

Question **A**nswer

Q1. What were prophets in the Bible?

A1. The biblical prophets were not fortune-tellers but _____ for God.

Q2. What two kinds of messages did the prophets speak?

A2. The prophetic message included _____ and _____.

Q3. What confidence can we have in prophecies not yet fulfilled?

A3. The accuracy of _____ fulfilled prophecies plus the character of God give us complete confidence that unfulfilled prophecies will be fulfilled.

For Further Thought and Discussion

1. What level of credibility have you previously given to self-proclaimed prophets in the media today? What credibility do you give them now?

2. What level of respect do you give to both aspects of prophesying, foretelling and forthtelling?

3. What level of personal confidence do you have that remaining prophecies, such as Jesus' second coming, will be fulfilled?

What If I Don't Believe?

If I don't believe in the credibility of biblical prophets and prophecies, I may have my confidence in the Word of God eroded, along with my hope in the deliverance promised to God's people in the future.

Also, if I don't believe in the *incredibility* of modern, self-proclaimed prophets in the media, I can get misled and confused by their prophecies.

For Further Study

1. Scripture
There are several Scripture passages which are important in studying this subject further. They include:

- Deuteronomy 18:10–12

- Deuteronomy 18:20–22

- Jonah 3:10

- Matthew 24:11

- Hebrews 6:18

2. Books
Other books are helpful in studying this subject further. They include:

Evidence That Demands a Verdict, Josh McDowell
Doomsday Delusions, C. Marvin Pate and Calvin B. Haines, Jr.

There can be no unity, no delight of love, no harmony, no good in being, where there is but one. Two at least are needed for oneness.
■ **George MacDonald**

12

What Are the Universals upon Which We All Agree?

Robert Frost once said, "The mind is a wonderful thing. It begins working the moment you wake up in the morning, and doesn't quit until you get to the office."

At times we could modify that to say, "The mind is a wonderful thing. It begins working the moment you wake up in the morning and doesn't quit until you start studying prophecy!" So it would seem when one undertakes a serious study of the subject. Not only do amillennialists disagree with premillennialists, not all amillennialists agree with other amillennialists, and not all premillennialists agree with other premillennialists. The uncertainties in the biblical text concerning prophecy make it impossible for us to agree for certain on what the Bible means in some cases.

This does not mean that we cannot be good friends and allies of people who hold to different positions than we do, as long as they are responsible positions built on a high view of Scripture. Covering the broad strokes, all else being equal, fundamental and evangelical amillennialists, premillennialists, and postmillennialists are brothers and sisters in Christ who share a belief in the character and power of God, the deity of Christ and the Holy Spirit, the inspiration of Scripture, the depravity of humanity, salvation by grace through faith in Jesus, and the responsibility to proclaim the message of salvation until Jesus returns. If we share that much in common, we are indeed members of one another in the body of Christ and responsible to "keep the unity of the Spirit in the bond of peace" (Ephesians 4:3).

There are people that we must keep a sharp eye out for, however, such as those who do not believe in the Trinity, or that Jesus and the

---

In this chapter we learn that . . .

1. We all agree that Jesus is coming again and that God will set all things right.
2. We all agree that Jesus is the ultimate focal point of all prophecy.
3. We all agree that holiness should be the end result of prophecy.
4. We all agree that we must be personally committed to the Great Commission.
5. We all agree that God is sovereign, and in spite of seeming evidence to the contrary, He is guiding history to a meaningful conclusion, just as He said he would.

Holy Spirit are God, or that the Bible is the inspired word of God, or that man is hopelessly lost, or that salvation is by grace through faith in Jesus, or that Jesus is coming again.

The ones we need to watch out for also include people who say that we are all gods, or who say that salvation comes by heightening one's latent god consciousness, or who believe in reincarnation. We need to be aware that the fastest-growing religion outside of Christianity is Islamic Fundamentalism, including in the United States. We need to be on the alert for Satan-worshipers, occultists, witches, and warlocks.

To be sure, there are valid areas of debate within fundamental and evangelical Christianity, and we cannot get lazy or lax in our "in-house" evaluation. Even brothers and sisters in Christ are capable of heresy. But we must also recognize the difference between those who are inside our gates and those who are outside. We must discern between responsible differences of opinion on the one hand, and apostasy and heresy on the other.

Why I need to know this

I need to know that there are vast and important areas of agreement among Christians so that I can respect those with whom I am in basic agreement and foster unity of the Spirit in the bond of peace.

For these reasons, I thought it important to close this book with a chapter on what we agree on, since the first eleven chapters are devoted largely to explaining the things that are not agreed on.

What Basic Prophecy Time-line Do We Agree On?

We all agree that Jesus is coming again and that God will set all things right.

In addition to the areas of doctrinal agreement mentioned above, there are four things regarding the future that fundamental and evangelical Christians agree on.

- First, we all agree that Jesus came the first time and that the message of salvation is entrusted to the church to tell to the world until Jesus returns.

- Second, we agree that Jesus will return at some time in the future to bring the fullness of the kingdom of God to humanity, and that there will be a new heaven and a new earth.

- Third, we all agree that there will be a time of judgment for Christian and non-Christian, with divine rewards for God's children and eternal destruction (realizing that term can be defined very broadly) for those who reject God. Each of us will be held accountable for how we lived while on earth.

- Fourth, we all agree that there will be an eternal union with God and with all of His children in heaven.

Some Christians would insist on adding much more to this future time-line. I understand. Even I would. But my point is that we would not want to take anything away from it. For me, it is the irreducible minimum on which we can all agree, and that minimum is significant in itself!

What Do We Agree upon Regarding Jesus' Relationship to Prophecy?

We all agree that Jesus is the ultimate focal point of all prophecy.

Under the umbrella of the glory of God, all things on earth, past, present, and future, look to Jesus. Jesus is the One to whom all past prophecies ultimately look. Jesus is the focal point toward which all future prophecies look. After the fall in the Garden of Eden, one great need dominated our lives: the need to have the sin problem corrected. We were cut off from God, separated from Him because of our sin, destined to eternal destruction. We were without hope. Paradise was destroyed, but God determined from the beginning to restore it. The focus on how Paradise would be restored is fuzzy at first, but it gets clearer and clearer until we see that Jesus is the way our sins are forgiven and the kingdom of God gets re-established.

All biblical prophecies ultimately point to Jesus. God promised to send a deliverer who would right this terrible wrong (Genesis 3:15). Then God got more specific, revealing that He would raise up a descendant from Israel, from the tribe of Judah (Genesis 49:10). Later He said that this descendent would be the heir to the throne of David (Isaiah 9:7), and that He would rule in righteousness and bring salvation to His people and to the world (Psalm 45:6–7; 102:25–27; Matthew 1:21; John 3:16). This is Jesus. And it is the figure of Jesus and the spirit of Jesus that is the focal point of all that God intends to do with humanity.

It is Jesus who will receive eternal praise for dying on the cross, for redeeming us, for making us kings and priests to our God to reign on the earth. Worthy is the Lamb who was slain to receive power and riches and wisdom, and strength and honor and glory and blessing . . . forever and ever (Revelation 5:9–13).

What Do We Agree upon Regarding the Purpose of Prophecy?

We all agree that holiness should be the end result of prophecy.

The bottom line regarding prophecy is that, while we may not know the exact makeup, sequence, and timing of future events, we are to plan as though Jesus were not returning in our lifetime but live as though He were returning tomorrow. We are to be at work, doing His will, manifesting His character, and proclaiming His name until He comes. The fulfillment of future prophecies must spur us to holy living as well as a diligence in ministry for the sake of those not yet redeemed.

The apostle John wrote:

And now, little children, abide in Him, that when He appears, we may have confidence and not be ashamed before Him at His coming. Beloved, now we are children of God; and it has not yet been revealed what we shall be, but we know that when He is revealed, we shall be like Him, for we shall see Him as He is. And everyone who has this hope in Him purifies himself, just as He is pure (1 John 2:28; 3:2, 3).

That is the key. Those who hope to see God will purify themselves, since God is pure. That is the point of prophecy. Not merely to satisfy our curiosity. Not to give us ammunition to win arguments with others over when Jesus is coming. It is to give us hope and to motivate us to live holy lives.

When prophecy is used to beat non-Christians over the head, when it is used to create animosity among Christians, when it is used as an interesting subject to be studied as an end to itself, then the purpose of prophecy is not being realized.

Biblical prophecy gives us hope and motivation for holy living.

I started this book by saying that when my wife, Margie, goes away on a trip, I let my housekeeping get a little casual. But when I remember that she is coming back, I want the house to be clean for her, and so I go to work straightening the place up. A major point of prophecy is to motivate us to keep our lives in order, so that whenever Jesus comes back we will have our houses in order. And if we die before He comes back, we will then have lived an honorable life.

What Do We Agree upon Regarding Prophecy and the Obligation to Evangelism?

We all agree that we must be personally committed to the Great Commission.

If we believe that we must all stand before God one day (Hebrews 9:27), if we believe that some people will be judged and sent to hell because they did not receive Jesus as their Savior (Revelation 20:11–15), if we believe that people must hear the gospel if they are to respond to it (Romans 10:13–15), and if we believe that Jesus has commissioned each of us to do what we can to spread the gospel (Matthew 28:18–20), then each of us must be personally committed to the Great Commission.

Just as each person who becomes a Christian reaches a point in which he must personally accept Jesus as his Savior and begin to live for Him, so there comes a point in each Christian's life in which he must accept playing his part in the Great Commission. He must recognize that he can no longer put it out of his mind and let others worry about it. He must be able to name something and say, "*This* is what I believe God is leading (has led) me to do to fulfill my responsibility toward the Great Commission."

We do not have the luxury of dismissing it as something for the "missions minded." We do not have the boldness to assume that God did not include us in the command. We do not have the freedom to turn our backs on those who have never heard and do nothing for them.

Certainly, we cannot all become foreign missionaries. That is not what we are all called to do. Someone in Los Angeles might be called to the forests of the Philippines to minister to a tribe of a few hundred people. Someone else stays in Los Angeles and ministers to some of the *millions* of people there who live without Jesus. Both contexts are mission fields. The question is not whether to go overseas. The question is: are we trying to reach the people God has called us to reach?

All Christians are called to do their part to fulfill the Great Commission.

Some people are called to interrupt a normal lifestyle to minister to the lost. Others consider the business world their mission field, which does not interrupt their normal lives. Rather, in the course of their everyday activities, they do what they can to try to share the gospel.

Christopher Parkening is one of the world's premier classical guitarists. Andrés Segovia, considered by many to have been the greatest classical guitarist of the twentieth century, said, "Christopher Parkening is a great artist—he is one of the most brilliant guitarists in the world."

Parkening was brilliant even as a teenager, and it was clear that he would be world-famous even at an early age. He made it his goal to make enough money to retire at the age of thirty, which he did. He bought a ranch in Montana that had a world-class trout stream, and he dedicated himself to his second love, fly-fishing. But his life soon became empty. Though he did not know what it was at the time, God was knocking on the door of his heart. Through the influence of the young woman who became his wife, Parkening committed his life to Christ and wondered what it was that God wanted him to do with his future. There were only two things he knew how to do: play the guitar and fly fish.

He decided that God wanted him to play concerts again, not for fame or money but as a platform to share the gospel, verbally, with those in the classical music world who are rarely exposed to the gospel. Today, Parkening is playing the guitar on the most famous stages of the world so that he can share the gospel.

Maybe you are a business person, maybe you are a homemaker, maybe you are a computer programmer, maybe you are a university teacher, maybe you are a construction or factory worker, maybe you are an artist. It doesn't matter what you are or where you are. There is a world God has called you to, and He wants you to go into that world and share the gospel.

God does not *need* you to do that. He can use another person to share the gospel. He could see to it that a person saw a Billy Graham crusade broadcast. He could use your pastor. No one will miss heaven because you were not faithful to share the gospel. But you will never be a complete Christian until you accept the Great Commission to take the gospel to others.

Doing one's part in the Great Commission does not have to be something heroic. My wife has taught me that. She will read a good book and say, "So-and-so would really benefit from reading that book." My response used to be, "Margie, so-and-so is not a reader. He's not going to read that big book." Her answer? "Well we know he won't if we don't give it to him." So, we buy the book and send it. And more often than not, so-and-so reads it! As a result of actions like this, a lot of people have become Christians.

I will never forget hearing one man talk about those whom he had led to the Lord. Someone asked him how he had been able to lead so many people to the Lord. He said, "I only talk to those who are interested in spiritual things." The response was, "How do you know who is interested in spiritual things?" To this the man replied, "I ask them."

"What do you mean you ask them? What do you say?"

"I say, 'are you interested in spiritual things?' If the person says 'yes,' we talk. If he says 'no,' we don't. One time I was driving down the freeway in L.A. and picked up a hitchhiker. When he had gotten in the car and we had exchanged names and so forth, I asked him if he was interested in spiritual things. He said, 'I've been searching for God all my life.' He came to Christ before I dropped him off."

I have talked to people who witness to people in airplanes,

and before the plane lands, every non-Christian has become a Christian, and every Christian has experienced revival. But

Our gifts and callings determine our roles in the Great Commission.

every time I share the gospel with people on an airplane, they either are already Christians, or they don't want a thing to do with it. The difference, of course, is gift and calling. We can't do what someone else is gifted and called to do, but we can do what we are gifted and called to do. I *am* not saying we must only be committed to something grandiose. I am saying we should ask God what He wants us to do to fulfill our part in the Great Commission. Then, as best we understand it, we do it. Until we come to that place in our Christian experience, we are not yet mature Christians.

Conclusion

God is often misunderstood. The world is a mess, and people don't understand why, if there is a God, He doesn't fix it. In fact, many wonder why He let it get into such a mess in the first place. When one looks at the chaos, violence, and random suffering that blanket the globe, it would be easy, on the surface, to dismiss God . . . to say that either He doesn't exist or, if He does, He doesn't have sufficient power or sufficient concern to make the bad things better.

Christians might have the greatest beef of all, because they believe they are God's children, yet they are not spared calamity because of it. In fact, many of them suffer even more because they are Christians, especially in communist and Muslim countries where being a Christian is a near or an actual crime.

God seems content to plod along (from our perspective), apparently letting the world run its course, yet asking His children to live a life that seems, on the surface, powerless against the forces of evil throughout the world.

In the meantime, He woos the world with love, relentlessly pursuing those who ignore Him or shake their fist in His face. Christians, of course, are His body . . . His physical presence on earth. He woos the world through us, so we have a great challenge to do a good job. He uses the weak things to overpower the mighty, and the foolish things to confound the wise.

At times we are blessed to see this strange way of God at work in the world succeeding before our eyes. Years of courageous faith, prayer, and witness by faithful Christians in Eastern Europe helped spur the downfall of the Soviet Union more than the Western press reported. Freedom from the scourge of communism grew from deep roots of faith that refused to shrivel and die in the rocky desert of militant atheism. Good overcame evil; the gospel of Christ proved stronger in all its apparent weakness than the antigospel of Leninist Marxism with all its apparent strength in bullets and gulags. The testimony of Jesus, which Revelation 19:10 calls "the spirit of prophecy," prevailed. The true freedom Christ always brings spiritually also produced a harvest of political freedom before the watching eyes of the whole world.

> **Sometimes we are blessed to see God's strange way of working in the world succeed before our eyes.**

In the middle of this amazing revolution of the spirit, Pastor Jerzy Popieluszko told his flock in Poland,

A man who bears witness to the truth can be free even though he might be in prison. . . . The essential thing in the process of liberating man and the nation is to overcome fear. . . . We fear suffering, we fear losing material good, we fear losing freedom or our work. And then we act contrary to our consciences, thus muzzling the truth. We can overcome fear only if we accept suffering in the name of a greater value. If the truth becomes for us a value worthy of suffering and risk, then we shall overcome the fear—the direct reason for our enslavement (quoted in *The Body*, Charles Colson 212).

These Christians were challenged by such truth and lived it, and whole nations fell under the weight of such truth. The church reflected God to the world, and the world could not hold the load. At times like this, regardless of our convictions about the time and nature of the Rapture or about the Millennium, we see God's movement in the world, and it is easy to believe that, yes, a day will come when "all the kingdoms of this world have become the kingdom of our Lord and of His Christ, and He shall reign forever and ever!" (Revelation 11:15). At times like this, we want to lift our voices and sing, bleat, or otherwise make a joyful noise (whatever each of us can do) with Handel's "Hallelujah Chorus."

Yet there are other times when we do not see God's strategy working. The annals of history are filled with Christians who died terrifying, meaningless deaths by the thousands and tens of thousands, and their lives have never been vindicated on earth. They are filled also with non-Christians who

In Eastern Europe, the church reflected God to the world, and the world could not hold the load.

were enslaved and sold or tortured and executed by their own leaders or slaughtered by violent conquerors. Whether Christian or not, these suffered unspeakable evil that we have never seen redressed. Justice continues to cry for satisfaction. The world continues to gasp with each contraction of evil's python-like grip on so many individuals and societies. Whether it is the image of the tow-headed ten-year-old boy dying slowly (too light to suffocate quickly!) on the gallows of a Nazi concentration camp or of the seven-year-old Rwandan girl orphaned by tribal massacres and now too weak from starvation to brush the flies from her dull eyes, anyone with a heart feels helpless outrage. If he believes in God, he cannot help but demand, "God where *are* you? Why aren't you *doing* something? How long will you let evil hold the day? When will you save us?"

These are the moments when Bible prophecy matters most. It matters because it tells us—through its overflowing treasure chest of fantastic images and promises, warnings and encouragements—that God will make everything right; that justice may seem deferred, but it will never be denied; that the good and gracious purposes for which God created the world shall all be fulfilled. Bible prophecy tells us that God is already at work fulfilling those purposes through Jesus Christ. Through Jesus, God has already entered the suffering of the world, already borne the world's sin, and already landed the knock-out punch on the devil and the evil he and human sin have jointly produced. Through the Resurrection of Jesus Christ, death itself has already been reversed and its paralyzing power of fear already disabled among those who receive the life of God here and now.

Bible prophecy goes further in assuring us that God will not leave the job half done, but He will continue to show how faithful He is, and He will complete the new creation begun in Jesus Christ. Because God is faithful, the Christ who now reigns over all of creation from heaven shall one day reign fully and visibly and without opposition on and over the whole earth. As part of

His reign, the victory of love over hate or apathy, of goodness over evil, of humility over arrogance, of gentleness over harshness, of kindness over cruelty shall one day be complete and completely revealed to all humanity. One day, the righteous, saving reign of God shall no longer be a matter of faith, but of full sight. And so the church of every age prays, "Even so, come, Lord Jesus!" (Revelation 22:20).

All students of Bible prophecy agree that prophecy tells us this. We disagree only on the *how* and the *when* of the details, and to some extent on the *who*—precisely how and when God shall consummate His kingdom on earth and whether or not the nation of Israel will be a significant end-times player. Discussion over these areas of disagreement is important and must continue with the spirit that befits brothers and sisters in Christ. But the differences must not divert us from our more significant agreements. And our agreements must not be only in statements of our beliefs. For the final important way Bible prophecy helps us is this: It assures us of God's ultimate victory in the world so that we better understand His purposes in the world and serve Him here boldly, with the confidence that comes from robust faith in His faithfulness.

Bible prophecy assures us that God will not leave the job half done, but . . . will complete the new creation begun in Jesus Christ.

When we hear Bible prophecy the way God wants us to, we do not stop with debates over which end-times time-line has it most right. Instead, because prophecy promises us that, after evil has run its course, God shall have *His* day, Bible prophecy causes us to ask, What should we, the body of Christ on earth, be doing now—at home, throughout our land, around the world?

What Pastor Popieluszko told Christians under the siege of a cruel dictator still helps answer this important question for us now:

Bible prophecy assures us of . . . God's future so that we may live . . . boldly today.

A Christian must be a sign of contradiction to the world. . . . A Christian is one who all his life chooses between good and evil, lies and truth, love and hatred, God and Satan. . . . Today more than ever there is a need for our light to shine, so that through us, through our deeds, through our choices, people can see the Father who is in Heaven (quoted in *The Body*, Charles Colson 213).

Bible prophecy helps us glimpse the certainties of God's future so that we may live wisely, righteously, passionately, and boldly today. It urges us, as we look for the coming of the Lord, to answer the question of 2 Peter 3:11: "What manner of persons ought [we] to be?"

Speed Bump!

Slow down to be sure you've gotten the main points from this chapter.

Question **A**nswer

Q1. What basic prophecy time-line do we agree upon?

A1. We all agree that Jesus is *coming again* and that God will set all things right.

Q2. What do we agree upon regarding Jesus' relationship to prophecy?

A2. We all agree that Jesus is the ultimate *focal point* of all prophecy.

Q3. What do we agree upon regarding the purpose of prophecy?

A3. We all agree that *holiness* should be the end result of prophecy.

Q4. What do we agree upon regarding prophecy and our obligation to evangelism?

A4. We all agree that we must be *personally committed* to the Great Commission.

Q5. What do we agree upon regarding prophecy and meaning in life?

A5. We all agree that God is sovereign, and in spite of seeming evidence to the contrary, He is guiding history to a *meaningful conclusion*, just as He said He would.

Fill in the Blanks

Question **A**nswer

Q1. What basic prophecy time-line do we agree upon?

A1. We all agree that Jesus is _____ _____ and that God will set all things right.

Q2. What do we agree upon regarding Jesus' relationship to prophecy?

A2. We all agree that Jesus is the ultimate _____ _____ of all prophecy.

Q3. What do we agree upon regarding the purpose of prophecy?

A3. We all agree that _____ should be the end result of prophecy.

Q4. What do we agree upon regarding prophecy and our obligation to evangelism?

A4. We all agree that we must be _____ _____ to the Great Commission.

Q5. What do we agree upon regarding prophecy and meaning in life?

A5. We all agree that God is sovereign, and in spite of seeming evidence to the contrary, He is guiding history to a _____ _____, just as He said He would.

For Further Thought and Discussion

1. What areas in your life would you want to see improved if you knew for sure that Jesus was coming back soon?

2. What would you have to do, or change, in order to say that you were fulfilling your part in the Great Commission?

3. When people see trouble in the world and are dismayed, what can you tell them when they wonder where God is?

What If I Don't Believe?

If I don't believe in the importance of focusing on the things that unify me with other fundamental and evangelical Christians, I may unnecessarily create disunity among other Christians. On the other side of the issue, I may miss out on the joy that could be experienced if I did focus on unity.

For Further Study

1. Scripture
Several passages in the Bible are central to studying this subject further. They include:

- Revelation 5:9–13

- 1 John 3:3

- Matthew 28:19–20

- John 14:1–3, 27

2. Books

Other books are helpful in studying this subject further. They include:

The Last Days Handbook, Robert Lightner
Friendship Evangelism, Joe Aldrich
Rediscovering Holiness, James Packer

Bibliography

Anders, Max. *What You Need to Know About the Bible*. Nashville: Thomas Nelson Publishers, 1996.

————. *What You Need to Know About the Holy Spirit*. Nashville: Thomas Nelson Publishers, 1996.

————. *What You Need to Know About Jesus*. Nashville: Thomas Nelson Publishers, 1996.

Crockett, William. *Four Views on Hell*. Grand Rapids: Zondervan Publishing House, 1992.

Dixon, Larry. *The Other Side of the Good News*. Wheaton, IL: Victor Books, 1992.

Elwell, Walter, A. *Evangelical Theological Dictionary*. Grand Rapids: Baker Book House, 1984.

Erickson, Millard. *Contemporary Options in Eschatology*. Grand Rapids: Baker Book House, 1977.

Habermas, Gary and Morgan, J.P. *Immortality, the Other Side of Death*. Nashville: Thomas Nelson Publishers, 1992.

Johnson, Carl. *Prophecy Made Plain*. Chicago: Moody Press, 1972.

Klein, William and Blomberg, Craig. *Introduction to Biblical Interpretation*. Dallas, TX: Word Publishers, 1993.

Lewis, C.S. *The Problem of Pain*. New York: MacMillan Publishers, 1944.

McDowell, Josh. *Evidence that Demands a Verdict*. San Bernardino, CA: Here's Life Publishers, 1979.

Mickelson, Berkeley. *Interpreting the Bible*. Grand Rapids: Erdman's, 1963.

Packer, James. *God Has Spoken*. Downers Grove, IL: InterVarsity Press, 1979.

Rawlings, Maurice. *Beyond Death's Door*. Nashville: Thomas Nelson Publishers, 1978.

————. *To Hell and Back*. Nashville: Thomas Nelson Publishers, 1993.

Tada, Joni Erickson. *Heaven, Your Real Home*. Grand Rapids: Zondervan Publishing House, 1995.

Walvoord, John and Zuck, Roy, *Bible Knowledge Commentary, Volume I*. Wheaton, IL: Victor Books, 1985.

Master Review

Chapter 1

Q1 What is prophecy?

A1. Prophecy is the predicting of *future* events.

Q2. Why study prophecy?

A2. We study prophecy not only to learn about the future, but also to have it *impact* our daily lives.

Q3. Why is there a strong interest in prophecy?

A3. There is a strong impression both among Christians and non-Christians that we are approaching the *end* of history on earth.

Chapter 2

Q1. What is creation?

A1. Creation is the *beginning* of the universe and human life.

Q2. What is covenant?

A2. A covenant is a binding *agreement* between two individuals, and God has embarked on a series of agreements with humanity.

Q3. What is Christ?

A3. Christ is the *fulfillment* of God's Old Testament covenant promises for Messiah to come to redeem humanity.

Q4. What is the church?

A4. The church is the totality of all *believers* in Jesus Christ who are to carry out His will on earth until He comes again.

Q5. What is the consummation?

A5. Consummation is the *completion* of God's eternal plan.

Chapter 3

Q1. Are prophecies to be understood literally or symbolically?

A1. Interpretation *varies,* and some prophecies should be understood literally while others should be understood symbolically.

Q2. Does each prophecy refer to only one event in history?

A2. Some prophecies had both an immediate and a *future* fulfillment.

Q3. What personal factors might influence different interpretations of prophecy?

A3. Factors such as upbringing, education, and *temperament* influence interpretation of prophecies.

Q4. How should we read and attempt to understand prophecy?

A4. We should read prophecy in its historical, grammatical and literary *context,* relying on the whole context of Scripture.

Chapter 4

Q1. What is the Second Coming?

A1. The Second Coming is the *return* of Christ to the earth at an unknown time in the future.

Q2. What is the Rapture?

A2. The Rapture is the sudden *departure* of all Christians to meet Christ in the air.

Q3. What is the Millennium?

A3. The Millennium refers to a period of time when Christ reigns in *righteousness.*

Q4. What is the Great Tribulation?

A4. The Great Tribulation is a period of intense, unprecedented *suffering.*

Q5. Who is the Antichrist?

A5. The Antichrist embodies evil and is the key *agent* of Satan's resistance to the plan of God in the last days.

Q6. What is the judgment seat of Christ?

A6. The judgment seat of Christ is the place where all *Christians* will receive their reward for the quality of their life on earth.

Q7. What is the Great White Throne judgment?

A7. The Great White Throne judgment is the place where all who have *rejected* God receive the punishment for their unbelief and their life on earth.

Q8. What are heaven and hell?

A8. Heaven and hell are the ultimate *destinations* of all people, depending on whether or not they truly believed in God.

Chapter 5

Q1. What is the Great Tribulation?

A1. The Great Tribulation is a period of intense suffering and divine *judgment* in the last days.

Q2. What is the pretribulation view on the Rapture?

A2. Pretribulationists believe the Rapture will occur *before* the Great Tribulation.

Q3. What is the midtribulation view on the Rapture?

A3. Midtribulationists believe the Rapture will occur in the *middle* of the Great Tribulation.

Q4. What is the posttribulation view on the Rapture?

A4. Posttribulationists believe that the Rapture will occur *after* the Great Tribulation.

Chapter 6

Q1. What is premillennialism?

A1. Premillennialism is the belief that the second coming of Christ will inaugurate a *literal* period of 1,000 years during which Christ will rule over the world as its political leader.

Q2. What is postmillennialism?

A2. Postmillennialism is the belief that the gospel will spread throughout the earth creating an increasingly *better* world after which Jesus returns to bring this age to a close and usher in eternity.

Q3. What is amillennialism?

A3. Amillennialism is the belief that the thousand-year reign of Christ is purely *symbolic* of the ultimate triumph of God's righteousness and goodness in the world.

Chapter 7

Q1. What is the judgment seat of Christ?

A1. The judgment seat of Christ is the place of *reward* for those who have accepted God while on earth.

Q2. On what basis are those who have accepted God rewarded?

A2. Those who have accepted God have already been forgiven for their sins and are now being rewarded for their good deeds and faithful *obedience* to God.

Q3. What is the Great White Throne judgment?

A3. The Great White Throne judgment is the place of *judgment* for those who have rejected God while on earth.

Q4. On what basis are those who have rejected God judged for sin?

A4. Those who have rejected God are judged on the basis of their *unbelief* and their thoughts, motives, words, and deeds.

Chapter 8

Q1. What happens when a person dies?

A1. When a person dies, his physical body ceases to function and his spirit *departs* to the spiritual realm for his eternal destiny.

Q2. What is the intermediate state?

A2. The intermediate state refers to human existence in the *interval* between a person's death and his resurrection to heaven or hell.

Q3. Who is resurrected from physical death?

A3. *Everyone* is resurrected from physical death, some to heaven and others to hell.

Chapter 9

Q1. What is the consensus view on hell?

A1. Hell is eternal *separation* from God and all that is good.

Q2. What is the literal view on hell?

A2. Literalists believe that hell is a place of endless, conscious, *physical*, spiritual, and emotional suffering in literal fire for those who have rejected God in their earthly life.

Q3. What is the metaphorical view on hell?

A3. Metaphoricalists believe that hell is a place of endless, conscious, emotional, and *spiritual* suffering for those who have rejected God in their earthly life.

Q4. What is the conditional view on hell?

A4. Conditionalists believe that hell is a place of conscious suffering for those who have rejected God in their earthly life, but which eventually *ends*.

Chapter 10

Q1. What is heaven like?

A1. Heaven is a place of unimaginable beauty and *joy*.

Q2. What will we do in heaven?

A2. We will *worship* God, reign with Jesus, and fellowship with one another.

Q3. What will we be like in heaven?

A3. We will be sinless *images* of the triune God.

Chapter 11

Q1. What were prophets in the Bible?

A1. The biblical prophets were not fortune-tellers, but *spokespersons* for God.

Q2. What two kinds of messages did the prophet speak?

A2. The prophetic message included *foretelling* and *forthtelling*.

Q3. What confidence can we have in prophecies not yet fulfilled?

A3. The accuracy of *past* fulfilled prophecies plus the character of God give us complete confidence that unfulfilled prophecies will be fulfilled.

Chapter 12

Q1. What basic prophecy time-line do we agree upon?

A1. We all agree that Jesus is *coming again,* and that God will set all things right.

Q2. What do we agree upon regarding Jesus' relationship to prophecy?

A2. We all agree that Jesus is the ultimate *focal point* of all prophecy.

Q3. What do we agree upon regarding the purpose of prophecy?

A3. We all agree that *holiness* should be the end result of prophecy.

Q4. What do we agree upon regarding prophecy and our obligation to evangelism?

A4. We all agree that we must be *personally committed* to the Great Commission.

Q5. What do we agree upon regarding prophecy and meaning in life?

A5. We all agree that God is sovereign, and in spite of seeming evidence to the contrary, He is guiding history to a *meaningful conclusion,* just as He said He would.

About the Author

Dr. Max Anders is a pastor at heart who applies the truths of God's word to people's everyday lives. An original team member with Walk Thru the Bible Ministries and pastor of a mega-church for a number of years before beginning his speaking and writing ministry, Max has traveled extensively, speaking to thousands across the country.

His books include the best-selling *30 Days to Understanding the Bible*, *30 Days to Understanding the Christian Life*, *30 Days to Understanding What Christians Believe*, as well as other titles in this series. He holds a Master of Theology degree from Dallas Theological Seminary and a doctorate from Western Seminary in Portland, Oregon.

* * *

If you are interested in having Max Anders speak at your conference, church, or special event, please call interAct Speaker's Bureau at 1–800/370–9932.